Do States Have the Right to Exclude Immigrants?

Political Theory Today

Christopher Bertram

Do States Have the Right to Exclude Immigrants?

polity

First published in 2018 by Polity Press

Polity Press
65 Bridge Street
Cambridge CB2 1UR, UK

Polity Press
101 Station Landing
Suite 300
Medford, MA 02155, USA

ISBN-13: 978-1-5095-2195-1
ISBN-13: 978-1-5095-2196-8(pb)

A catalogue record for this book is available from the British Library.

Library of Congress Cataloging-in-Publication Data

Names: Bertram, Christopher, 1958- author.
Title: Do states have the right to exclude immigrants? / Christopher Bertram.
Description: Cambridge, UK ; Medford, MA : Polity Press, [2018] | Series:
    Political theory today | Includes bibliographical references and index.
Identifiers: LCCN 2017054073 (print) | LCCN 2018006640 (ebook) | ISBN
    9781509521999 (Epub) | ISBN 9781509521951 | ISBN 9781509521968 (pb)
Subjects: LCSH: Emigration and immigration--Government policy. | Border
    security--Government policy.
Classification: LCC JV6271 (ebook) | LCC JV6271 .B48 2018 (print) | DDC
    325/.1--dc23
LC record available at https://lccn.loc.gov/2017054073

Typeset in 11 on 15 Sabon by Servis Filmsetting Ltd, Stockport, Cheshire
Printed and bound in the United Kingdom by Clays Ltd, St ives PLC

For further information on Polity, visit our website: politybooks.com

Contents

v

Acknowledgements

Many thanks to the friends and colleagues who have discussed material or ideas that have found their way into this book. Many of the good ideas are theirs, the bad ones are down to me. Some are sympathetic to the arguments presented here, others are not. They include Diego Acosta, Rutvica Andrijasevic, Chris Armstrong, Richard Ashcroft, Zara Bain, Megan Blomfield, Harry Brighouse, Joanna Burch-Brown, Natasha Carver, Katharine Charsley, Helen de Cruz, Speranta Dumitru, Sarah Fine, Tim Fowler, Jon Fox, Matthew Gibney, Melanie Griffiths, Patti Lenard, Matthew Lister, Sylvie Loriaux, Eithne Luibheid, Yasha Maccanico, Alejandra Mancilla, Macarena Marey, Cara Nine, Kieran Oberman, David Owen, Pauline Powell, Devyani Prabhat, Arthur Ripstein, Alex Sager, Nandita Sharma, Ann Singleton, Martin Sticker,

Acknowledgements

Anna Stilz, Denise Vargiu, Alice Pinheiro Walla, Helena Wray, Lea Ypi, my editor George Owers, two anonymous readers, and three years of students on my Ethics of Migration and Citizenship course at Bristol. I have also profited enormously from reading the work of other scholars on the ethics of migration. Foremost among these is undoubtedly Joseph Carens, whose *The Ethics of Immigration* is deservedly the most influential work in the field. My father, Peter Bertram, died when this book was in preparation; I miss his love and the confidence that he always had in me.

Introduction

Immigration is one of the most controversial topics in politics today. In the United Kingdom, anxiety about immigration helped propel the vote to leave the European Union in June 2016. In the United States, concerns about immigration from Mexico and Central America featured strongly in Donald Trump's successful bid for the Presidency. In 2015, forced migration, in the form of hundreds of thousands of people seeking safety from conflicts in Syria and other parts of the Middle East, became central to the European political agenda, with some political leaders calling for a compassionate response to the crisis while others claimed that the flow of 'genuine' refugees was mixed with 'economic migrants' searching for a better life. Some of these movements were new, but many continued patterns dating back decades or longer. Though readers are probably most keenly aware of the migration events I have mentioned, they are only the most newsworthy parts of the picture. Other countries and regions, such as Russia and South Africa, experience strong inward migration and sometimes social tensions as a result. Many movements of people, such as of nurses and domestic workers from the Philippines to wealthy countries, or of construction workers from Nepal to the Gulf States, get much less publicity.

When politicians discuss immigration, they usually stress the costs and benefits to 'us', the settled electorates of the nations in which they are running for office. Politicians from the populist right play to fears about change, about threats to national cultures, about incomers with different religious beliefs, about crime, or about competition for jobs and supposed downward pressures on wages. In countries where economic growth has slowed, where there are many people who have not benefitted from globalization and where living standards have suffered from tight fiscal policies, foreigners, particularly visible ones, are an easy and obvious target for resentment. By contrast, more market-oriented politicians argue for the benefits of immigration: 'our' economy needs skilled migrants. 'We' need our companies, schools, universities and hospitals to hire the best people for the job, irrespective of their passport. Skilled immigrants can help plug vital skills gaps in sectors like health, social care and construction.

Despite deep differences on both facts and principles, politicians and commentators from the populist right, the 'neoliberal' centre and the traditional left share the assumption that immigration policy should be determined by what 'we' need. This book is not about whether immigration is beneficial or harmful to 'us'; it is about something more fundamental. It is about whether states have the *right* to exclude immigrants and whether people have the *right* to migrate and make new lives in countries other than those of their birth or nationality. Politicians, commentators and members of the general public who frame the immigration debate in terms of costs and benefits to 'us' assume that the state (and democratic electorates) have the right to set immigration policy pretty much as they choose. Indeed, states do have the *legal* right to do just that. But this book argues that the legal rights states have need moral justification and cannot be taken for granted.

Most of us appreciate the difference between what we personally like and what we have a right to do. I might prefer it if the people coming to live in my part of town shared my economic background or cultural or religious view. It might be better for me if more people like me moved in. It would boost house prices or lead to more shops or restaurants in the local area catering to my tastes. But I have no right (legal or moral) to exclude people different from me from my area and it would be wrong to use personal or political pressure to do so. The right to regulate migration is not so different from the right to decide who can settle in your locality: whatever right there might be to do such things needs justification.

Normative theorizing about migration is likely to encounter resistance from a number of sources. For politicians, policy-makers and many members of the general public, questioning the assumption of state discretionary control can seem absurd and outlandish, particularly where their horizon is fixed by the policy agenda, or by what the electorate might tolerate in the near future. Engaging with politicians and policy-makers can also be dangerous and distorting for the normative theorist, because the pressure to be 'relevant' to policy concerns often means that conversations proceed from a tacit assumption that policy-makers' beliefs about the state's right to control are justified. Discussion often shifts to helping policy-makers achieve their aims and away from any questioning of the basic legitimacy of those goals.

Activists and social scientists working on migration often have the opposite assumption, namely that all restrictions are bad, and that the state and its officials should be resisted at every turn. Sometimes such a view is based in explicitly anarchist convictions, but often it stems from a close and bitter experience of how states function, and how they damage the lives of vulnerable people. A primitive sense of justice and injustice can be a pretty good guide in the world of immigration policy and enforcement. Such people are wary of arguments that could *ever* justify state controls, because they think of such justifications as providing ideological cover for what actual states do when the moral imperative is rather solidarity with the oppressed and disadvantaged. I hope this book can persuade both camps that normative theory has something to offer.

The argument has three parts. The first is mainly descriptive: I discuss some aspects of the current migration, border and citizenship regime, how it came into being and its main characteristics. This is necessary because discussion too often takes place against a background of problematic beliefs about migration, the state and the citizen. Nation states, the entities who are trying to 'control' their borders, are institutions of fairly recent invention and are neither the natural nor the normal things that they are often thought to be. Many of the particular nation states that exist have boundaries artificially superimposed on much older patterns of ethnic, economic, social and family interaction. The persons who live on the territory over which these states exercise jurisdiction are not all citizens in good standing whose status as 'British', 'French' or 'Indian' is an uncontroversial matter of fact. Rather there have always been large numbers of people who 'don't fit', legally, socially or both. And the current regime of border controls and its documentary accompaniment of identity cards, passports and visas is of very recent invention.

The second chapter is the most theoretical. It asks how we should think about the right to regulate migration and what could justify it. It draws on an insight from the eighteenth-century German philosopher Immanuel Kant, who argued that when we claim a right to a thing or piece of land, we thereby also claim to impose a duty on others not to use it without our permission. Why should they respect our claim? Why is it morally acceptable to use force or threats to enforce it against them? Kant's answer is that it is wrong to use force *unilaterally* against others and that rights and duties have to be justifiable from a perspective that both the right-holder and the duty-bearer can share.

In this spirit I ask whether the existing norms around migration that give states an (almost) unlimited discretionary right to exclude are justifiable to everyone: citizens of wealthy countries and poor ones; sedentary citizens and would-be immigrants. I ask which norms might be and argue that rules that could be justified to everyone would permit much more freedom of movement than we have now but that ultimately we need global institutions to adjudicate the various claims and values from a perspective that is fair to everyone.

In the third chapter, I shift focus from the global and universal to the standpoint of particular states and individuals in a world like our own. There is often a difference between first-best solutions that assume that everyone is complying with fair principles and the second-best policies that we should follow when they do not. I ask about what individuals and states should do in an imperfect world where some states are determined to pursue unjust policies no matter what. I argue that individual states should do two things: first, they should make good faith efforts to work with other states to bring a more just global regime into being; second, in their current policies they should anticipate at least the minimal standards of such a regime. They must respect and protect the human rights of immigrants and they should bear perhaps more than their fair share of migration costs, even if they are not obliged fully to compensate for the injustice of other states. Where states act reasonably justly in this way, then citizens and would-be immigrants also acquire some duties towards them to comply with their rules; where states do not act justly then immigrants do not have to obey their immigration rules or give truthful answers to their officials, and citizens must work to change unjust policies and mitigate their effects.

1

Migration Today and in History

Much popular and political thinking about immigration assumes that an international order based on dividing the world into nation states, in which places belong to peoples and each individual has their naturally allotted location, is the normal order of things. Not only is it 'normal', but it is also normative, a state of affairs from which deviations must be justified but which is not itself in need of justification. This distorts our thinking about human migration and mobility. Nation states are recent historical creations and the invention of a world order based around them is within living memory.

This chapter explains the normative assumptions about membership and place embedded in the global order and says something about the real effects that the enforcement of this order has. As a counterpoint to this 'normality', I first say some general things about the nature and history of migration before discussing the nation-state form and the way in which states distribute membership. I then enumerate some of the effects of doing things this way and discuss the refugee regime as an apparent anomaly. Setting out something of the reality of a world in which nation states have, with limited exceptions, discretionary control over migration provides a background to my later discussion of what a just system for the international regulation of migration might look like.

Who are the migrants?

If you ask the typical person in the United Kingdom or the United States about immigration, they may think of poor people crossing the Mediterranean Sea in flimsy overcrowded boats or of Mexicans trying to evade the barriers on the southern border of the United States. Other common images are of non-white people living in deprived urban areas, running small businesses or in low wage jobs. Often, citizens of wealthy countries will be concerned about such people coming 'illegally' and the threat that they could pose to jobs or public services. These images represent the immigrant as 'other', often Muslim, and a threat to 'our' way of life.

Of course, there are desperate people trying to make dangerous journeys, some are non-white and some are Muslim; but despite the visibility of particular representations of immigrants in tabloid newspapers or in television documentaries, such images are not representative of migration as a whole. Most migrants who move across borders do so to settle in ways authorized and even encouraged by states. They may be pursuing economic opportunities, moving to study, uniting with family members, seeking a place in the sun to retire to, and yes, in a minority of cases, fleeing from war or persecution. In other words, they are usually ordinary people, moving from one location to another, for ordinary human reasons. Many of the people thought of as 'immigrants' in the popular imagination are not even immigrants at all, but citizens or legal residents, born and raised in the country where they live.

The latest international figures indicate that in 2015 there were about 244 million international migrants in the world, that is to say, people living outside their country of origin.[1] Of these, just under half were women. The average migrant was 39 years old. Of the total migrant stock in the world, 51 per cent lived in ten countries, the most popular being the United States with an immigrant population of 46.6 million. The country with the largest diaspora was India, with 15.6 million of its nationals living outside its borders. Immigrants make up a much higher proportion of the population in some regions than in others. In Latin America and the Caribbean, the proportion is low, at around 1.5 per cent, but in Europe it is higher (10 per cent) rising to 17.5 per cent in Austria. Unsurprisingly, a settler state like Australia has a high proportion of foreign-born residents (28 per cent) but the numbers in the Gulf states, which include large numbers of temporary workers with few rights, are staggering, rising to 88.4 per cent of the population in the United Arab Emirates.

Migrant workers (150 million) make up the majority of the world's stock of migrants. Refugees, at 21.3 million, are a much smaller proportion of the total, though they only constitute a minority of the world's forcibly displaced persons, most of who remain within the boundaries of their states of origin. The International Organization for Migration estimates that around 50 million of the total are 'irregular' migrants, although given that much irregular migration is clandestine by its very nature, reliable figures are hard to come by. Though there is a widespread perception that migration has increased in recent years, this is true only in absolute terms as the proportion of migrants in the world population has not changed much over the past fifty years (it is currently 3.3 per cent). What has changed is the pattern of migration, with European countries, once a major source of emigration, turning into receiving countries and their populations becoming more diverse as a result.

Why do people migrate?

What makes people migrate? The folk theory that most ordinary people, journalists and politicians probably believe is an economic one. The idea is that people want to maximize their wealth and income and will move to a new place if they believe this will make them financially better off. This contains a kernel of common sense: where people can choose between alternatives that are similar in other respects, and one brings more money than the other, they will usually choose the one that pays better. Using this simple notion, and noticing the great inequalities between wealthy countries in Europe and North America and the global south, people often conclude that, given the opportunity, nearly everyone from a poor country would leave. Perhaps many people would. But we should be wary about endorsing some of the more apocalyptic scenarios, because money is not the only thing people care about.

In reality, people want a range of different things, many of which are tied to particular places and social networks such as family and relationships, religion and community, culture, language, cuisine, landscape and climate. A decision to migrate might bring someone more money, but it also risks severing them from many other things they value. Ironically, many people who worry about mass migration out of fear that immigrants will disrupt rooted communities and dilute local culture, often ascribe to hypothetical immigrants a set of purely financial motives which they think of as not applying to themselves.

We can see how ineffective economic motives are against the incentives to stay provided by family and culture by looking at states and groups of states within which relatively free movement coexists with large disparities in economic opportunity. People from the poorest places do not automatically uproot themselves and move to the richest ones. Within the United States, for example, there are large disparities between wealthy areas, particularly

14

on the coasts, and poorer regions in the South and Appalachia. Yet most people remain within their state of origin, and this in a country with a shared language and culture where the costs of moving are fairly low. According to a 2009 report, 57 per cent of US residents have not lived in the US outside their current state and 37 per cent are still in their home town.[2] In the European Union, though there has been migration from poorer member states in the east to wealthier ones in the north and west of the continent, most people stay put, preferring the familiar to the new. In 2015, fewer than 3 per cent of residents were nationals of another EU member state.[3] Over time, small movements can add up to much larger shifts in population, but the idea that discrepancies in wealth lead to immediate stampedes has little support.

What can make large numbers of people move in a short space of time is when conditions become intolerable where they are and they have little hope of maintaining their existing forms of work, life and family. The kinds of catastrophic events that cause such movements are hard to predict, but they include natural disasters, famine, war and persecution. The most recent such movements of which people in wealthy countries are aware were those following the Arab Spring and during the war in

Syria. Such events usually happen in poor countries, which are often ill equipped to cope. Though the causes of many crises are linked to the past policies of wealthy states, most of the people who move end up in similarly poor countries in the same region.

Migration in history

Migration is a pervasive and normal part of the human experience. Our earliest ancestors, themselves migratory hunter-gatherers, left Africa and spread across the planet, and human beings, individually or in groups have been moving ever since. But perhaps the important recent watershed in human mobility comes in 1492, with the 'discovery' of the New World by Columbus. The destruction of the native populations of the Americas through warfare and disease meant that European colonists had to find new sources of labour to exploit their new territory and, through the Transatlantic slave trade, colonial powers imported whole new populations, mainly of black Africans, to work for them under terrible conditions.[4] European colonists spread across the planet, seizing the lands of indigenous people and often destroying their societies or pressing them into servitude, and later founding new colonial-settler states like the United States, Australia and Argentina. In the nineteenth century European states, bolstered by ideologies of racial supremacy, conspired among themselves to divide up territories in Africa where no European had ever trod. Meanwhile, millions of poor Europeans, from places like Scandinavia, Ireland and Italy, were encouraged or driven by poverty and lack of opportunity at home to start new lives in the Americas or the Antipodes, a process that continued into the twentieth century.

In the period after the Second World War, things changed again. North-west European states underwent a rapid economic transformation, with a growing population, many of whom were still too young to work, and high levels of economic growth. As a result, these countries sucked in labour, initially often from their southern European neighbours, but in the case of colonial powers such as the United Kingdom, France and the Netherlands, their overseas subjects. Many of these workers faced tough conditions and lived in poor housing with insecure rights to stay, but they eventually constituted a significant proportion of the workforce. In the UK, citizens of the Empire were initially free to enter without restriction, and some industries worked hard to recruit workers from places including the West Indies, but by the end of the 1950s there were signs of rising intolerance among the white population and nationality criteria and entry requirements were progressively revised from the 1960s onward. In addition to immigrants from the Caribbean, Britain's population of South Asian origin also increased, particularly after Idi Amin expelled the Ugandan Asians after 1972. In France and the Netherlands, similar stories can be told of how members of subject colonial populations in places including West Africa, the Maghreb, the Antilles and Indonesia came to live, work and settle in the former colonial metropolis. As a result of these changes, many West European states shifted from being countries of emigration to countries of immigration, and their racial and ethnic composition changed dramatically.[5]

In the United States the picture is slightly different, since it was historically a country of white settler immigration (as well as forced migration of Africans), but one bordered to the south by Mexico. Early limitations on immigration were aimed at non-whites. The Naturalization Act of 1790 limited US naturalization to 'free white persons' of good character. Notoriously, Chinese settlers in California were targeted by the Chinese Exclusion Act of 1882, which stopped the entry of Chinese workers and barred their naturalization. Many of the south-western states were established on territory that formerly belonged to Spain or Mexico and which contained a population of indigenous and Hispanic ancestry whose social, family and cultural connections spanned the new border, and immigration from Latin America (and Canada) was not subject to a numerical quota. Mexican workers were, however, subject to occasional deportation drives throughout the twentieth century. The policy changed in 1965, when the United States abandoned its country-based immigration system which had aimed at preserving the ethnic proportions that existed in 1920 among Americans of European origin. The political price of moving away from a system that favoured white Europeans was a closing of the border to the south and the creation of a 'problem' of 'illegal' immigration from Mexico and other Latin American countries.[6] The effect of the abandonment of national quotas has been ultimately to change the character of the United States by making it also a much more ethnically diverse society.

It would be possible to repeat elements of this story for a variety of different wealthy liberal democratic states. The short version, however, is to say, that despite different histories, many such states have, through processes that partly involve migration, acquired quite diverse populations.

The nation state as a container

This internal diversity is in tension with one of the central organizing principles of the modern world, the nation state. The most important fact about the modern world that distinguishes it from earlier forms of society from the perspective of human mobility is the dominance of the modern state, with its centralized power, codified legal systems, defined citizen body, clear territorial jurisdiction and, more recently, public health and welfare systems. In the twentieth century, a particular conception of the state, linked to the idea that peoples or nations realize their self-determination through each having their own state, became globally dominant. Virtually the whole landmass of the earth is now subject to state authority. By contrast, until recently states only ruled over parts of the earth's surface, and many people lived in stateless areas beyond their borders.[7]

The proliferation of the national form of the state has its origins around the time of the French Revolution. But the link between the idea of a sovereign people and an ethno-cultural conception of 'the people' really took off with the 1848 revolutions in Europe and found institutional realization in a multiplicity of new nation states after the dismemberings of the Austro-Hungarian and Ottoman Empires after the First World War. This process also created a 'problem' of national minorities trapped within the borders of states that aimed to achieve someone else's idea of self-determination. During the Second World War, Hitler and Stalin further advanced the ethnic homogenization of the states of Europe through the destruction or displacement of those same minorities. The Second World War hastened the proliferation of the European nation-state model to the rest of the world through the beginnings of decolonization and the creation of the United Nations and the post-war international legal order.[8]

Although many of the newly decolonized states were, in fact, multi-ethnic and multi-linguistic, the dominant normative idea of the international order was and is that of a series of juridically equal states, each with their own 'people'. On this model peoples, through their states, exercise territorial sovereignty, are supposed to guarantee the human rights and basic needs of their citizens, and enjoy collective rights over the minerals and other natural resources that fortune has placed on their territory. Although some peoples, such as the Kurds, lack their own states, they are seen on this model as anomalous. In principle, each person has a home state where they belong, to which they owe allegiance and which has responsibility for them. The world therefore appears as a series of juxtaposed containers, each being a little moral universe of social co-operation, with a place in an appropriate container for each person.[9]

There are many discrepancies between this neat juridical picture and social and economic reality. First, far from reflecting the actual networks of social intercourse, post-colonial boundaries often cut across them, so, for example, Bangladesh, literally 'the state of the Bengalis', is severed from the dominant city in Bengal, Kolkata, as a result of a border created at partition, with potentially deadly consequences for those who wish to maintain family or economic relationships by crossing it.[10] Second, while, the containers may be formally equal sovereign states, they differ enormously in economic value, in political character and in relative power. Some states end up being the subordinates and clients of others and formal popular ownership of natural resources often translates into pillage and theft by companies based in wealthier nations. Some individuals are lucky enough to find themselves born into wealthy and stable countries and are dramatically advantaged compared to those who are not. Third, many of the individuals present on the territory of states and subject to their laws are legally, socially or culturally not citizens or members of the dominant group.

The regime of discretionary choice

The international norms governing migration and citizenship are essentially that states have the right to decide whether or not to admit migrants for work or settlement or for any other reason and have broad discretion on how to set their laws on nationality and citizenship. Most people get their nationality at birth by some combination of two criteria. Some states grant citizenship to any babies born on their territory (known as *ius soli*, or law of the earth), whereas others regard citizenship as something to be passed down from parents to children (*ius sanguinis*, or law of blood). Each of these methods taken alone has major defects because they risk excluding from citizenship people who will probably live their lives under the laws of the relevant state; so most states combine the two principles in some way or other.

Where states do exclude large numbers of natural-born residents, the act of exclusion may well be deliberate. For example, Latvia framed its citizenship law in historic *ius sanguinis* terms to deny membership to the children of ethnic Russians who had settled on the territory during the period of Soviet control. Myanmar notoriously excludes from membership most of the predominantly Muslim Rohingya minority. By these methods, the vast majority of people in the world grow up with the citizenship of some particular state rather than being cast into the limbo of statelessness, in which no government recognizes a duty to look after their basic rights and interests. Some people even end up with more than one citizenship, perhaps being born to Italian parents (a *ius sanguinis* jurisdiction) on the territory of a country like the United States, which grants citizenship on a *ius soli* basis.

In addition to these forms of birthright citizenship, some – including many migrants – acquire citizenship of a particular country in later life. This is usually by a process known as naturalization, which may depend on length of residence and on meeting other criteria of integration or linguistic competence. Naturalization is fairly cheap and easy in some jurisdictions and hard to impossible in others. To those who acquire citizenship through birthright and those who go through regular natu-ralization processes, we can add the super-rich, who have the option of simply buying themselves the citizenship of states, either directly or by being put on a fast-track to naturalization after investing a large sum of money.[11]

Differential value of citizenships

As mentioned above, some people are much more advantaged by their citizenship than others. If you are born with the nationality of a state such as Burundi, your life-chances are worse than someone born with the citizenship of a country like Belgium. A citizen of a wealthy country usually has better educational facili-ties and medical services and access to labour markets with more lucrative opportunities than someone from a poor country. Indeed, economists believe that between-country differences in wealth and income are a more important source of inequality between individuals than within-country differences.[12] If you want to be well-off, or even have your most basic needs and human rights protected, it is a good idea to choose the country of your birth carefully.

These inequalities in the value of the nationalities people receive at birth are exacerbated by migration and naturalization regimes based on state discretionary choice. If you are a wealthy person from a poor country or have significant marketable talent or training, you can often escape the country of your birth and join a richer society because you will be seen as a potentially valuable asset. Conversely, a poor and unskilled person from a poor country is likely to be locked into the social and political infrastructure they were born within because, though they have the legal right to leave, wealthier countries will not admit them.

Some theorists have compared these inequalities in the value of a heritable status to pre-modern regimes such as European feudalism and the Indian caste system, where some babies were born with the proverbial silver spoon in their mouths and others looked forward to hardship, toil and subordination.[13] Today we find it offensive to our ideals of freedom and equality that some people within a state should inherit a formal legal status that is near-impossible to change but which locks them into permanent disadvantage. Yet, while most affirm the idea that all human beings are equal in moral status, in the sense that they have equal basic rights and that they have no greater entitlement to having their needs catered for than anyone else, we live in a world where inherited national citizenships ensure vast inequalities of life chances and economic outcomes.

Though there is a tension in practice between universalistic ideals and inegalitarian reality, we should not draw the conclusion that it is inevitable. In principle, a more even distribution of global wealth and income and a universal respect for human rights would mean that someone's life-chances would not be greatly affected by the happenstance of their birth nationality. Unfortunately, though, development economists seem to have little idea how we might bring about a more equal regime in practice and even how we might rid ourselves of some of the most egregious poverty.[14] Foreign aid projects, for example, are often wasteful and ineffective. There is evidence, however, that allowing more migration does make poor people from poor countries better off, both by giving them access to labour markets where they are more productive and because of the money transfers they make to their place of origin, the volume of which greatly exceeds all the foreign aid payments in the world.

Immigration and the national-liberal tension

The discretionary immigration admission policies of nation states highlight a tension between

27

the liberal commitments of states and their ethnonational character. Insofar as they are liberal, states are committed to protecting the basic rights of their members, respecting those of non-members, and providing a framework of rights and resources to enable their members to pursue their goals and ambitions. Using the state as a vehicle for the promotion of ideals and values that only some citizens share, is, on a liberal view, hijacking an instrument that belongs to everyone on behalf of the sectional interest of some. Put simply, liberalism suggests that immigration and citizenship policies, like other policies, should be neutral as regards the ethnic, religious or racial characteristics of would-be immigrants.

On this liberal view, what matters for immigration policy is public benefit, and the kinds of things that are relevant are mainly whether immigrants will help society by making economic contributions such as plugging skills gaps. What seems unacceptable is that a liberal state should run a migration and citizenship regime that explicitly favours people from some particular race or ethnicity over others, such as Australia did with its 'White Australia' policy in much of the twentieth century.[15] Where a state already has citizens from a variety of different racial and ethnic backgrounds, it disrespects some of them and undermines political equality if it pursues an immigration policy that makes clear that 'people like them' are less desirable than people of the dominant race or ethnicity. Even if a state entirely lacks members of an excluded group, it is hard to see how an explicitly exclusionary policy aimed at a particular race is consistent with judgements about the moral equality of human beings that any state formally committed to human rights has officially made.

The real-world incentives facing political leaders in a nominally liberal democratic state with a dominant ethnic group often point in a different direction. Citizens from the dominant group will be electorally crucial and may conceive of the state as 'theirs' in the sense that it belongs to and should further the interest of the nation in the ethno-national form in which they imagine it. Consequent electoral pressures will often favour somewhat restrictive immigration policies that give migrants who are relatively similar to the in-group priority over those who are not. What often happens in such cases is that supposedly neutral rules are devised which give a veil of deniability to immigration rules that disproportionately affect some ethnic groups rather than others. For example, the family migration rules in the UK have used criteria such as income, language competence and genuineness of relationship in ways that are easier to satisfy for white Britons in relationships with, say, white Australians, than for people from ethnic minorities with lower average incomes who want to marry partners from Pakistan or Bangladesh. Though there is nothing explicitly racist about the policies as formulated, the impact is markedly skewed.[16]

Many policies around the 'integration' of immigrants also have this dual character. On the one hand, there is nothing obviously objectionable about policies that help everyone to play a full part in society. Being able to speak the dominant language tolerably well and to navigate the often unspoken conventions of social life are desirable skills if people, including new immigrants, are to take their place as equals among others. On the other hand, such policies often take the form not of providing practical assistance to people who would otherwise be marginalized, but rather of presenting barriers which immigrants close to the dominant national group will pass with ease but which exclude those who speak a different language or do not share the habits, customs and values of the majority. Such barrier-like 'integration' policies also tell people in the core national group that the state has their interests and their conception of the nation at heart, and that official toleration of minority groups is strictly limited.

People who don't fit

A pervasive effect of the migration and citizenship regime is the creation on the territory of the state of categories of person who fail to fit neatly into the container model of states and citizens and often lack full and effective membership of the states where they live. Some of them are nominally citizens, but on worse terms than native-born citizens from the dominant group. These include naturalized citizens vulnerable to citizenship deprivation and people whose voice is diminished because they belong to minority groups or groups of immigrant origin. Others are people such as non-citizen family members of citizens, those whose presence is conditional on some kind of transnational citizenship (such as EU citizenship), foreign permanent residents, foreign students, people with temporary work visas, asylum-seekers and refugees, irregular migrants who have arrived as adults and persons who have been born or brought up on the territory but who have, by legal accident or deliberate policy, been denied full membership of the state.[17] To these we should add members of groups distributed across different states and where family and social relationships require cross-border access, such as the Kurds or the Roma of central Europe.[18]

This is a large and heterogeneous collection of people. A few are immensely privileged and have a high degree of effective power, but many more are poor and marginalized. Some, such as EU nationals in the UK before the Brexit referendum, feel entirely secure in their status, not worrying about the possibility of it being undermined until the unthinkable happens. Others will be more immediately conscious of their vulnerability. Many members of these groups will struggle to access vital services as easily as citizens can, some of them will be at risk of removal or deportation if their circumstances change. Often they will find it difficult to make long-term plans because their right to stay is uncertain. Beyond the individuals who comprise this group stretches a penumbra of others who enjoy full citizenship but whose interests are deeply intertwined with those of more vulnerable status: family members, friends, work colleagues and others.

For some of these cases it might be possible to mitigate the problem by restoring or improving the fit between those living on the territory and the state's membership, perhaps by making it easier for people who are in practice members of a society to acquire political rights or citizenship, as philosophers such as Joseph Carens have urged.[19] This would certainly be an improvement over the status quo. But the discretionary norm means that the acceptance of any such proposal by states is likely to be patchy. In Italy and Switzerland, there has been widespread opposition to suggestions that citizenship rights be extended to those born on the territory. And even if such a change were to secure widespread acceptance, there would still predictably be large numbers of people, such as temporary labour migrants, living and working in a country other than that of their nationality, who would lack effective representation.[20]

In a world in which the international migration regime emerges as the result of the combination of the unilateral discretionary actions of states around border control and membership definition, the voices that are likely to be dominant will be those of the insiders who constitute the majority of each state's population. Pretty much all of the people who fit neatly into the container model and who identify squarely as members of their particular state will be within the democratic public of those states which are democracies. By contrast, many of the people who do not fit will be denied representation within the states in which they live and work, and will perhaps be denied representation anywhere, despite working, paying taxes and being subject to law. In the UK, for example, perhaps 1 in 10 of the workforce are in this position.[21] A lack of democratic representation for many such people means that politicians have no incentive to take their interests into account but will rather give more weight to the views of the native and sedentary population, including on the issues where those who do not fit are most sharply affected.

Effects of the border regime

Maintaining the ideal of the nation state as a container for 'its' citizens and enforcing the regime of state discretionary choice requires states to control movement of populations and to deny access to valuable social resources to people who lack the right status. States police their external perimeters to reserve access to the physical space to citizens and others who have permission and try to prevent unauthorized persons from making use of labour markets, health and welfare services.

These state borders are places of violence and coercion. The daily struggles between migrants and border guards from Calais, from the US–Mexican border, around Spain's African enclaves of Ceuta and Melilla and in southern and eastern Europe are perhaps the best-known examples. States have erected physical barriers, threatened 'illegal' entrants both with immediate violence and with legal penalties, imposed fines on airlines who transport people who lack the required documents, and exposed those who try to evade their restrictions to exploitation and abuse in places like Libya and Mexico and horrible death in deserts and on the sea. As well as constructing formidable physical barriers, states have invested heavily in technology to detect human movement in border zones and have promoted militarization of their border control forces, creating a windfall for companies that supply the equipment and technologies. Beyond their borders, wealthy liberal states have also enlisted the support of more repressive regimes through agreements to prevent people from departing from or travelling through their territories, at considerable cost to the human rights of the would-be migrants.[22] Such methods make life difficult for many migrants, but they also aim to prevent refugees fleeing from persecution from being able to arrive on the territory of states to claim asylum.

Though what happens at and beyond the physical

borders of states often provide the most dramatic scenes of confrontation between states and migrants, measures within the territory of states are also of great importance and can have a corrosive effect on their internal life and political character, often in ways that are invisible to 'ordinary' citizens.[23] 'Hostile environment' regimes, such as checks on employment or measures to prevent housing being let to irregular migrants, can worsen life even for citizens who resemble the presumed irregular immigrant population in race, ethnicity or accent, reinforcing divisions among citizens between those who are perceived as being 'normal' and others whose effective legal citizenship status is weakened by a perception that they are not. Attempts by governments to act effectively against irregular migrants in the light of populist pressures can come into conflict with human rights obligations and legal protections, giving rise to political pressure to weaken such safeguards. The division of immigrants themselves into categories of desirable and undesirable and the demands to deport 'foreign criminals' can also lead to a weakening of equal protections and the rule of law, as governments try to deprive people of access to effective legal remedies. Even citizenship itself can be undermined as a unitary category when governments seek to strip undesirables of their citizenship in order to reclassify them as foreign and force them from the territory, a risk that only some citizens, usually naturalized members, are exposed to.[24]

Where governments attempt to impede irregular migration by imposing duties on law enforcement, social services, doctors, schools, or even private citizens to report those they suspect of immigration offences, they risk harm both to the immigrants themselves and to the wider society. People suffering from communicable diseases may not seek medical help if they fear their immigration status will be disclosed, and pregnant women may not seek timely assistance, putting their child at risk. Children may be deprived of education at a crucial point in their development if parents fear that schools will share information with immigration enforcement. People housed in substandard or dangerous accommodation will be reluctant to inform the authorities if doing so risks exposure, increasing the probability of events like the Grenfell Tower fire disaster in London in 2017. Irregular migrants will be less willing to report crime, either as victims or witnesses, if the police will also arrest them for immigration offences, meaning that serious criminals may get away with their crimes and vulnerable migrants are prey to exploitation. Developments like Sanctuary

Cities in the United States are an attempt to respond to some of these problems by setting up what Joseph Carens has called a 'firewall' between immigration enforcement and other services, but they only achieve partial coverage and are constantly under political attack.[25]

Even those 'legally' present on the territory are exposed by the discretionary migration regime to onerous risks and burdens. For example, many migrant workers find themselves in very precarious employment and social conditions. If they are factory workers or agricultural labourers, for example, they are often part of a flexible reserve, employed through agencies rather than directly, and liable to be taken on or laid off as economic conditions change, with no stable employment rights. If they are domestic workers, they are often invisible and isolated in the home of their employers, liable to work extremely long hours and sometimes subject to visa restrictions that link them to the particular job they are in and therefore make the prospect of dismissal catastrophic. Such conditions of dependence put the employer in a dominant position and make such workers extremely vulnerable and liable to exploitation and abuse, including sexual abuse and violence.

Finally, the immigration enforcement regime

weakens the rule of law because of the way that it puts enormous discretionary power into the hands of officials. Border officials or civil servants issuing visas make judgements about whether individuals are visiting a country for the purposes they claim, such as tourism or study, or whether they have some ulterior and unauthorized purpose. Officials make assessments of whether marriages are 'genuine' or have been entered into to evade immigration control or whether asylum applicants are credible. The officials who make these judgements are often stressed and overworked and are themselves often under performance regimes that reward hitting arbitrary targets to get the numbers down. The decisions such officials make are often questionable and are sometimes based less on evidence but on prejudice against whole categories of applicant. Liberal states are supposed to replace the capricious rule of men with the impartial and predictable rule of law, but in the case of immigration, they fall well short of this ideal.[26]

Persecution and the refugee regime

The significant apparent exception to the norm that states have the discretion to reject whoever they like at the border is the international law regime govern-ing refugees. States who have signed up to the 1951 Geneva Convention on the Rights of Refugees and its 1967 protocol accept a duty of *non-refoulement*, which is a duty not to expel persons fleeing per-secution back into circumstances where they face persecution. They also have obligations to assess the claims of people who seek asylum according to the criteria set out in the Convention and to recog-nize as refugees those who meet them. The criteria are that a refugee is someone who is outside his or her country of nationality or habitual residence and who has a 'well-founded fear' of persecution on the basis of a number of protected characteristics: 'race, religion, nationality, membership of a particular social group, or political opinion.'

The Convention has its roots both in the desire that such shameful failures of the 1930s that ulti-mately contributed to the Holocaust should never be repeated and in the practicalities of dealing with displaced persons after the Second World War. During the Cold War, it also provided the framework under which Western powers provided sanctuary to those escaping the Warsaw Pact countries, and was hence a sign of commitment to democratic and liberal values.

The Convention regime for refugees does not

contradict the view of nation states as containers, but rather seeks to remedy the problems that arise when the system of nation states fails to do its job. Hannah Arendt famously observed that citizenship was the right to have rights,[27] meaning that the human rights of people who had found themselves stateless in the inter-war years had been rendered empty because states were only willing to provide effective protections for their own citizens and not for foreigners. The legal status of refugee, enshrined in the Convention, aims to give people outside of their designated container an internationally recognized status that can substitute for their ineffective or severed nationality and can set them on the path to the acquisition of a new one.[28]

In practice, the Convention has often not worked well. Electorates of Western democracies who were prepared to accommodate those fleeing communism have proved less tolerant of those escaping conflicts in Africa, Asia and the Middle East. Many of those who have claimed asylum have been demonized as 'bogus' by politicians and the press, with the suggestion often made that the asylum system is a loophole permitting economic migration. Since the obligation of states are towards those who present themselves on territory within their jurisdiction, states have often done their best to ensure that people fleeing persecution never reach their borders.

The Convention, with its focus on persecution, often interpreted differently in different countries, also fails to offer protection to many people who common-sense would suggest have a valid claim to protection. Living in a war zone where your children risk a stray bullet on the way to school is not grounds for refugee status and nor, for many countries, is forcible conscription into the military of a vicious dictatorship. Direct threats from state officials may get you protection, but it will be harder to make your case if those you fear are private militias or criminal gangs. The Convention does not cover those displaced by natural disaster or climate change, though the impacts of natural disasters may fall disproportionately on minorities whose interests the state neglects, and those displaced within the borders of their country of nationality have no right to international protection.

When those fleeing persecution do present themselves for asylum, their troubles are hardly over. They face a long wait to have their claim assessed, are often denied the right to work and may have to live on very meagre public support such as the £5.32 per day they get in the UK. Their claim may be treated with disbelief, with the least inconsistency held up as evidence of deception in ways that are now thought to be outrageous in dealing with citizen victims of trauma such as rape. Claims are often rejected after poor decision-making by officials, and asylum-seekers can then face a daunting and long appeals process.

Some will achieve refugee status in their country of asylum and be put on a path to full citizenship in that country; others whose valid claims have been recognized, will nevertheless be removed to some offshore quasi-prison and told that they will never make that transition, as is the case with many people who have tried to make the journey to Australia by boat. In the United Kingdom, refugees are now re-evaluated after five years and if the country they fled is deemed by Home Office officials to be 'safe', they may be removed there, even though the country may be far from safe by any reasonable standard. This prospect of removal adds to the stresses on a group of people who already face greater mental health burdens, disincentivizes them from integrating and makes it less likely that will be given long-term employment.

Most people fleeing persecution never make it to the territory of a signatory state. Rather, most refugees end up in states near to conflict zones such as Kenya, Pakistan, Turkey or Lebanon. Some of these people are in camps managed by the United Nations

High Commissioner for Refugees, where they often live miserable and constricted lives and many others eke out an existence in the towns and cities of those states. Some of the cost of supporting people there is borne by wealthy countries and those wealthy countries sometimes resettle people directly from those refugee camps. Sometimes representatives of wealthy states appeal to the fact that they resettle refugees or give extraterritorial support as evidence that they are playing their part and, indeed, this is a contribution. However, if we look at where the vast majority of refugees end up, it is hard to resist the conclusion that most of the costs are met by the poor countries where the majority of refugees live and by refugees themselves when they are denied protection or are forced to endure harsh conditions.

Conclusion

Depending on how we look at things, the container version of the world either realizes or conflicts with the moral commitments of liberalism. This is because liberalism is committed to the idea of a polity of free and equal persons subject to law. Within the container, or at least within those containers that have achieved a liberal order, freedom and equality characterizes the relationship among citizens in theory. But since not everyone on the territory is a citizen, and as there are also persons beyond the boundaries of the state, what appears as a regime of equality can actually be one of inequality, as some people have more rights than others.

This might not be such a problem if the global system of containers worked as advertised and corresponded to the underlying social reality. If every person had their appropriate place within an overall system of states, then each person could participate in relations of freedom and equality locally with their fellow citizens, and every person everywhere could enjoy adequate protection for their vital interests and human rights, thereby achieving equality with all others in the sense that everyone enjoys protections and opportunities that meet some standard of adequacy.

Needless to say, our actual world looks nothing like this. Not only are the containers of very different value to one another, but even the putative equality that is supposed to obtain within them is often endangered by inequalities beyond their borders. Many people simply do not fit neatly as they supposedly should, and they and their friends and family often experience subordination and vulnerability as a result. In the next chapter I consider how we might think about a regulatory regime for migration that is justifiable to everyone rather than being the summative effect of the discretionary choices of nation states.

2

Justifying a Migration Regime from an Impartial Perspective

This chapter asks about which norms should ideally govern human mobility. It is followed, in the next one, by a different question: given that we live in a world that falls well short of being just, what should our attitudes and policies be now? In this chapter I argue, first, that the norms governing human mobility, including mobility across borders, have to be justifiable to everyone (and that ultimately, justification requires some institutional embodiment). Second, I argue that the current norm, that states have an almost unqualified right to regulate immigration as they choose, cannot meet that test. Third, I claim that some limitations on human mobility might be justifiable from a perspective that everyone can share. The central idea of the chapter is an idea about rights and duties that is inspired by Immanuel Kant, namely that there is a difference between might and right, and that claims of right, in order to be other than mere assertions of power against others, have to be justifiable to everyone. When states claim the right to control their borders and to exclude immigrants, they are also saying that those immigrants have a duty to respect that right. Should we accept this claim or is the exclusion of outsiders a naked imposition of power that outsiders may be forced to accept but which they are not morally obliged to?

What states claim

In the modern world states claim the right to control their borders. That is, they claim the right to decide who crosses the border, who can settle in the country, and who has the right to work there. They also claim the right to decide who, if any, of the people that they allow to settle in the country may acquire the rights of political membership or citizenship, and they assert rights to do things such as removing or deporting foreign nationals from their territory. States claim that they have these rights as an aspect of their sovereignty, and hence not requiring negotiation and compromise with others. This is the norm of unilateral state discretion over migration discussed in the previous chapter, a right qualified only by a few caveats about refugees and the general human rights of migrants. When states claim the right to exclude, they are not simply saying that they have the effective power to keep unwanted foreigners out. In fact, to a greater or lesser extent, that is a power that all states fail to have, since all states have some people present on their territory without authorization. Rather, they are claiming that they have, as a matter of justice, the right to keep those people out.

Rights of this kind, sometimes called 'claim rights', are rights that logically entail duties on others. Property rights are one form of claim right and can serve as an example. If I own a bicycle, that ownership right implies that you have a corresponding duty not to take and use it without my consent. States in claiming a right to exclude also thereby assert that others, foreigners, have a duty not to enter or settle on the territory without authorization. In recent years, many states have reinforced this view of the 'illegality' of unauthorized entry and settlement by explicitly criminalizing it and making it nearly impossible for the unauthorized to live and work on the territory without committing criminal offences. In the eyes of the state, those people are doing something wrong for which they may be justly punished.

Obligation and the closed society

The state's claims to impose rights and duties on its territory are essential to what it is as an entity. The claim to be the sole source of authority within a particular geographical space both characterizes the state and marks it as distinct from other and earlier forms of human political organization.[1] When trying to think about the justification of that authority and about issues of what a fair society looks like, political theory and political philosophy have often looked at states as if they were sealed-off units, unrelated to the world beyond their borders and with a population consisting entirely and exclusively of members of that state's 'society'.[2] In this respect, states and societies as abstractly considered by political philosophers bear a resemblance to the ideal container model of nation states considered in the previous chapter.

Taking states as closed societies, the key questions that arise concern the relationship between the state and the people who live on the territory and are subject to its authority. These questions are largely about the source and nature of that authority. What could make it legitimate (if anything)? What form may legitimate institutions take? How must the co-operative structures organized by the state function and with what results if they are to be just or fair to citizens? The central claim that states make with respect to their territory and the people on it, is that they have the right to command people to act in various ways and that people have a duty to obey. States claim the right to establish various rules and to punish violators, to appropriate the resources of their citizens via taxation and the work of their bodies via conscription.

These claims are extraordinary. As a private person, I have no right to subject my neighbour to my commands, to inflict punishment, to seize her assets or to make her perform labour to advance my purposes.[3] In fact, were I to do such things I would face sanction at the hands of the state and its agents. Since I, as an individual, lack the moral authority to subject my neighbour to my purposes, it can seem mysterious that a group of people – a human community – could have or acquire the right collectively to exercise an authority that none of its individual members has.

The German philosopher Immanuel Kant tried to answer the question of how people could impose duties on one another through an adaptation of the social contract theory developed in different ways by earlier thinkers such as Hobbes, Locke and Rousseau. Like Hobbes, Kant thought of the alternative to state authority as being a 'state of nature', a stateless condition in which we could not enjoy security of our persons or possessions. He argued that individuals who found themselves in such a state of nature would be under a natural duty of justice – that is, a duty binding independently of and prior to conventions or agreements – obliging them to enter into a law-governed state with other people who happened to live nearby. When a group of neighbours enters into this new way of living together, they reject relationships that amount to each person trying to force others to comply with his or her will and agree to be bound by a set of rules that are justifiable from a public perspective that is common to them all. Instead of social life being a battle in which the stronger parties subdue the weaker ones, people abide by conventions that treat them all fairly and which they can all endorse. For Kant, this was not a matter of anything that happened historically, but rather a way of understanding what the state both essentially is and ought to be: namely, a mechanism for establishing impartial justice that works in everyone's interest.[4]

To put it mildly, it is often a stretch to fit this way of thinking to what happens in actual states. Most of us live in highly unequal societies where access to political power is not fairly distributed but where people with greater wealth or status have more of it. As a result, the system of rights and laws can look like what Marx thought it was, an instrument for the better-off to advance their interests at the expense of those who have less wealth, prestige or education. Still, if the Kantian story were successful, it could help justify and explain some of the relationships we find ourselves in within law-governed societies, where people feel themselves obliged to play by the rules and respect the rights and property of others.

The important moral idea to keep hold of from this 'Kantian' approach is that nobody should simply impose their will on someone else, unilaterally dominating them and limiting their freedom and autonomy, but that we should rather seek to establish arrangements within which such limitations on freedom as are necessary for us to live together in the world are decided on in a way that is fair to everyone, and respects their equal status as moral persons. It is easy to see that from this perspective, the situation of would-be immigrants is radically different from that of co-nationals.[5] In a state that meets reasonable standards of fairness and reciprocity, fellow nationals experience limits on their individual freedom and autonomy. But they should be able to accept those limitations as fair and reasonable because the same conditions are applied to everyone, and they are necessary conditions if everyone is to get by together in society. The rules gain their authority over us because of considerations of fairness and reciprocity. It would not be right of me to force rules on you that I am not willing to accept myself. There is a kind of implicit bargain here, a *quid pro quo*, that gives each person good reason to accept the rules.

But while this theory might have some attraction as applied to the relations among people who live together under a law they have jointly made on the territory of the state which they inhabit, it is going to be in difficulties as soon as we change the picture to include other states, people who live outside the territory, people who want to enter the territory and settle on it, and people living on the territory who lack the right to take part in the making of the rules. This is because those people stand outside of the implicit bargain that reciprocally binds citizens in the ideal case.

A natural extension of the theory might be to suggest simply absorbing those human communities and individuals into the existing law-governed arrangement, establishing a new public perspective that includes them.[6] After all, if we are under an obligation to enter into law-governed relations with people we are unavoidably living next to, then the fact that they are just beyond the boundary of an existing territory might suggest that we just need to incorporate them in the scheme of justice we are already part of. In principle, such a process might go on until everyone in the world was subject to a world state. Kant himself resisted such a conclusion, but he did think that we needed to think about some international public mechanisms so that relations, both among states and between residents of particular countries and foreigners, could be regulated fairly and in the interests of everyone.

The need for an impartial perspective

The question we need to ask, then, is which norms concerning the relations between insiders and outsiders, between states and immigrants, between human communities of citizens and would-be entrants to them, could be justified from a standpoint common to them all? Political and moral philosophers have developed a range of tools for thinking about issues like this. The Scottish philosopher and economist Adam Smith, for example, advanced the idea that to see the world morally is to have the capacity to see one's own actions and those of others, not just from the perspective of one's own interests and passions, but as they might appear to others without a direct stake in the matter and, ultimately, in the eyes of an 'impartial observer'. The American philosopher John Rawls made famous the idea that principles of justice are principles that would be chosen from behind a 'veil of ignorance'.[7] Philosophers such as Joseph Carens writing on the topic of immigration have already adapted Rawls's device to the issue and I propose to follow their lead to ask what kind of rules governing human mobility and settlement across state borders we could justify (or at least reject as unjustifiable) from an impartial perspective.[8]

Veil of ignorance

Rawls asks what principles people would choose to govern society if they had to choose those principles without knowledge of their personal circumstances, strengths, weaknesses, ambitions, commitments or tastes, and then had to live in a society governed by the principles they chose. The idea is that if people are prevented by ignorance from designing society in ways that reflect their own abilities and proclivities, they will be led to choose a system that is fair for everyone. Rawls's treatment of the choice issue in *A Theory of Justice* is both controversial and highly technical. It is also bound up with his views about the metaphysics of moral principles. I intend to use the idea here in a much less ambitious manner, namely, simply as a heuristic device to help us to think about which norms and principles concerning migration could be acceptable to everyone and which could not be.

How should we use the idea of the veil of ignorance to think about migration? One possibility is that we simply ask what rules people would choose to govern migration if they were deprived of knowledge of their nationality. We can imagine each of the world's passports being placed in a barrel and people being invited to settle on some principles to govern global immigration before blindly putting their hand in the barrel and pulling out a passport. The randomness of the choice would mimic the mere happenstance of being lucky enough to be born with entitlement to a particular nationality in the actual world, where the beneficiaries of powerful nationalities such as the birthright citizens of the United States or Germany have done nothing special to get their privileges over those unlucky enough to be born in Burkina Faso or Uzbekistan.

Depriving choosers of knowledge of their nationality is not enough on its own because even those with nationalities that are disadvantaged in the actual world can easily overcome that disadvantage just so long as they have other assets such as wealth or talent. Like Rawls, then, we must also deny our choosers knowledge of their native abilities and their social position as well as normally unchosen characteristics such as sex, race and ethnicity. We must also deny them knowledge of some of their tastes and preferences, attachments and proclivities so that they cannot tailor their choice of migration norms to suit their own private goals. But while depriving them of knowledge of their particular likes and circumstances, we should provide them with general knowledge of things that are essential prerequisites for living a decent life.

Any list of such prerequisites is inevitably going to be controversial and I cannot settle such controversy here. Rawls tries to address the issue via his idea of primary goods, presumed to be useful to any rational plan for life, and by a ranking of some primary goods, rights and liberties, as being of overriding importance compared to others, such as wealth and income, because of the close connection of rights and liberties to our interests in autonomy and religious freedom. Another way of specifying such a list is via the capability approach associated with Amartya Sen and Martha Nussbaum. Here, the idea is that people should have capabilities to access certain key 'functionings' central to the possibility of a decent human life. Nussbaum provides a list of such core capabilities which includes such things as an expectation of normal human life expectancy, of good health, nourishment and shelter, of being secure against violations of bodily integrity and having reproductive choices protected, of having opportunities for the exercise of one's intellectual, imaginative and emotional capacities, of being able to associate with others under conditions where self-respect is possible and one is not exposed to humiliation, of being able to play and enjoy the natural world, having opportunities to shape political and economic choices.[9] The satisfaction of some such interests is a matter of degree and may well involve trade-offs between different dimensions of human experience. But it seems reasonable to think that people would not want to expose themselves to the risk that they would be thwarted in one or more of their most core interests if a set of conventions to govern global migration that did not expose them to such risk were available.

Let us imagine, then, four possible sets of rules to govern global migration. The first of these is unilateral discretionary choice, where states, as a function of their sovereign power, have full authority over whether to admit or deny entry to would-be immigrants. The second is a modification of state discretionary choice to form more of a global system: in other words something like the global system of nation states as containers for peoples, with state discretion hemmed in to some extent by the refugee regime and by international human rights law. This would be a system that had been 'cleaned up' somewhat compared to the status quo, in other words a global regime where states took their human rights obligations seriously instead of trying to evade them as they do now. The third is a regime of open borders under which people are free to cross international borders and resettle at will. The fourth is a regime with a presumption in favour of free movement, where any restrictions on free movement have to be justifiable according to criteria acceptable to everyone and where there is a representative set of institutions to interpret such principles and adjudicate disputes.

Possible migration regimes

1. Unilateral state discretion

The current regime of state discretionary choice would not be chosen from behind a veil of ignorance. The reasons for this should not come as a surprise, given the account of some of the failings of the actual system in the previous chapter. Simply put, it exposes far too many people to the risk that they will be thwarted in pursuit of their most vital interests. The acute differences in expected wealth, educational outcomes and life expectancy that people face as a result of global inequality mean that people would not opt for a system where they would be at risk of being locked into a social and economic environment bearing those disadvantages. Somebody choosing in ignorance of their political and religious affiliations but knowing that in some locations they might be the target of political or religious persecution would not choose a regime which made it difficult for them to escape that persecution and which exposed them to serious dangers of rape, murder, hunger, thirst or drowning in the way that the current system does. If a person knows they might be gay but that there are countries where homosexuality is persecuted, they would not choose a migration regime that forced them to stay and hide their sexuality or prevented them from fleeing their homophobic persecutors. A person conscious that they might turn out to be the parent of a child, the child of elderly parents needing care, or the romantic partner of another human being, would not choose a system of discretionary choice where states could impose hard-to-meet restrictions such as the UK's minimum income requirements for family and spousal visas. People would also avoid arrangements for membership or security of residence that left them at risk of deportation and thereby made them vulnerable to exploitative employers.

2. A modified status quo

Still, perhaps we should not immediately conclude that this unilateral restriction of their freedom is unjust. Particular states, after all, form part of an international system of states which usually recognize various norms and restrictions on their conduct (international law), including the right of states to control their borders. One possibility, then, is that the norm of state discretion, though it might look like the application of one-sided decisions against outsiders, could be justified from a perspective that everyone can accept. Just as property laws within particular states are justified from a standpoint that is common to all citizens, so the territorial control of states and their right to control their borders could be justified similarly. Something like the container model, cleaned up and improved could on this view provide the basis for a just system of global migration.

This model also has the property of being congruent with a commonly held view within political philosophy, which takes the individual state as the basic unit within which social co-operation takes place, starting from the assumption of a closed society in which all those present on the territory and subject to law are citizens, and then approaches questions which cross borders – like trade, migration, international human rights and climate change – as being matters for agreement among these discrete political units which have primary responsibility for protecting the basic rights and ensuring the well-being of their own citizens. On this view, while states' primary responsibility is toward their own citizens, they also have responsibilities to respect the human rights of those outside their borders and perhaps to step in and protect those human rights in the case where rogue states are violating them. And perhaps such states also have residual responsibilities to ensure that people living beyond their borders are not living in such dire poverty that they cannot sustain institutions of their own: a cleaned up container model would ensure minimal standards are met everywhere.[10]

We should not be too quick to dismiss this possibility. The period over which the modern state has become the dominant form of political organization has also been one in which human productive power has grown enormously and along with it levels of individual prosperity, and where – despite appalling episodes of war and genocide – levels of interpersonal violence have declined compared to earlier periods. If states are indeed to be credited with these good consequences and with corresponding increases in human freedom, and if the norm of state discretion is constitutively necessary for states to achieve such ends, then such a norm might be one that everyone has reason to accept. If everyone is better off and freer in a world governed by a system of states in which states have the right to exclude compared to the alternative of statelessness or anarchy, then the right of states to exclude, though limiting the freedom of would-be immigrants, still leaves them freer (and richer) than they would otherwise be.

The key objection to this view of a system based on discrete states as forming the background to a just global migration regime should be clear from the previous chapter. The view sets out as a normatively privileged model of global interaction a conception within which interests that do not fit neatly are addressed as afterthoughts in a tidying-up process. In reality, it is not the case that states have arisen separately as self-contained little moral and co-operative universes and have only later decided to engage in cross-border interaction. Rather, state borders in the actual world are overlaid on and cross-cut with patterns of co-operation and attachment which often pre-exist the formation of modern states. The point here is not just or even mainly a historical one; it is that by presenting the container system as the norm, we also make more salient than is justified the interests and identities of some people rather than others while making the interests of 'the people who don't fit' less visible, or even invisible. In allowing a global migration regime to emerge from discussion and agreement among states, the container model privileges the voices that get heard within states: the solid citizen from the dominant ethnicity, the median voter. The voices of those whose vital interests transcend state boundaries, such as the person with family or economic relationships with foreigners are somewhat muted. The interests of those without representation in the system, such as temporary labour migrants and those whom the vagaries of citizenship law have excluded from the electorate, are silenced.

3. Open borders

Another possible rule, the very opposite of state discretionary control, is to say that there should be no regulation of migration at all and that people should be free to move wherever they like, whenever they like. Sometimes people use the phrase 'open borders' to denote this sort of international migration regime, at other times people talk about there being no borders. I shall not discuss fine distinctions here: the basic idea to keep in mind is one where there are no legal barriers to individuals crossing state boundaries to make new lives for themselves. State boundaries might continue to exist, but they would separate units whose function was mainly administrative, in the same way as the borders between US states or local authority boundaries are today. Fully open borders can look like an attractive ideal, particularly compared to state discretionary control, because it leaves people free to escape the very risks that state discretionary control exposes them to and allows individuals to associate together for whatever purpose they choose.

The prospect of open borders, though, often meets with very fierce opposition, particularly from members of sedentary populations in wealthy countries who fear the arrival of very large numbers of outsiders. This opposition has many different grounds, but important among them are concerns about resources, worries about labour market competition and worries about changes in the cultural character of the places where such settled people live. These reasons are often presented in the context of arguments for unilateral state discretionary control, in other words as conclusive arguments why states should have the right to control immigration. But presenting such reasons as conclusive may lead us to neglect an important possibility, namely, that they have some provisional validity that we have to take account of in an all-things-considered global system. It seems plausible that they do. To give but one example, there will be limits on the number of people who can sustainably live in some ecologically fragile areas of the planet. We probably want to keep the population of those areas below the level at which serious damage is done, so long as we can do so without compromising some value or interest of even greater urgency.

If the parties to our veil-of-ignorance thought experiment were constrained to choose from just three options – unilateral discretionary choice, a system of nation states, and open borders – they would surely pick open borders, since open borders carries the lowest risk of catastrophic harm to them. But the possibility of a fourth option exists which includes a presumption in favour of free movement and, hence, against exclusionary restriction. It shifts the burden of proof away from the would-be immigrant and onto the state. But many reasons that might justify exclusion are not thereby silenced. What is needed, both as a practical matter and as a matter of justice, is a system of adjudication that takes into account the interests of all seriously affected parties so that in the event that someone wishes to migrate onto the territory of a state and that state wishes to prevent them on some particular ground, the claims of the contending disputants can be judged fairly.

4. A global procedural system

The central objection to states excluding would-be immigrants at will was that it constituted a unilateral imposition of a duty in a way that could not be acceptable from a perspective that both the right-holder and the duty-bearer could share. This made it unlike, say, exclusion from private property within the context of a state, because there, the framework of rights could be justifiable to all subject to it. We have seen that there is no way of saving state discretion from a more universal standpoint: people placed behind a veil of ignorance would not choose a norm of state discretionary control because of its threat to their basic interests. The final possibility to be considered here combines the feature that it is plausibly choice-worthy from behind a hypothetical veil of ignorance with an attempt to introduce something like justification to everyone in the real world.

Obviously, the barriers to institutionalizing a system of justification to everyone at a global scale are formidable. One way of doing so would be to introduce a global state, but there are good reasons to think that as well as being impractical, a global state is also undesirable because of the inevitable distance that would exist between it and any global public. Kant worried that it would either collapse into anarchy or be a distant tyranny. Even a partial system of democratic justification, according to which everyone would have a say in the norms of a global migration regime, looks impossible to organize.[11] Yet an alternative of merely liberal justification, according to which some philosopher or political theorist devises a set of norms for global mobility and explains why everyone has a good reason to accept it, also seems unsatisfactory. Of course, philosophers and political theorists have a role to play, and this book aims to be part of that conversation, yet the task of devising a fair migration regime that is justifiable to everyone would inevitably have to draw on the expertise of people from a wide range of different disciplines and professions, with their specialized knowledge, but also on the concrete experience of ordinary people from different continents and countries, and particularly of those who have suffered the worst effects of the current system such as refugees, those forced to make dangerous journeys, those placed in precarious positions of 'illegality' and those separated from loved ones.

In my view, the most plausible form such a regime would take would involve an international convention arrived at after discussions that would involve a range of different actors, including states, NGOs and a representative selection of affected persons, including, most importantly, migrants themselves. The convention would establish a set of principles that would include both a presumption in favour of free movement and a set of reasons why free movement might be overridden in particular cases. The convention would also harmonize principles of membership and citizenship so as to avoid the dangers of statelessness and to provide everyone with a guarantee of effective membership at their location. Once agreed, such a convention might best be administered by some kind of representative international adjudicatory agency that would decide on claims to restrict free movement. What can we say about the substantive content of this convention, given that such a regime is one that would secure effective representation of and justification to the interests of the full range of human beings affected by it, within the limits of practical possibility?

First, we can say that the burden of proof within such a system will fall on those who want to make the case for exclusion. Although immigrants do make some impositions on the communities they enter, notably in exposing them to positive duties of assistance, the most significant imposition is the one involving the exclusion of the person who wants to enter. We know that exclusion can endanger significant interests people have in being able to shape their lives as they wish, in being able to associate freely with friends and family, in being able to pursue economic opportunities, and indeed in escaping serious threats of persecution and poverty. States or other human communities wishing to exclude persons would have to demonstrate that the reasons for which they sought to exclude outsiders were sufficiently important to outweigh the interests of those individuals in free movement and that they could not reasonably satisfy those important reasons by other means.

Second, we can say something about citizenship and membership. What is important here is that people who make their lives at some location and within some social network possess an effective set of legal rights to protect their basic interests and to shape the social environment within which they find themselves. So if somebody is resident on the territory of a state for a period of time, or works on the territory of the state, they need a bundle of rights that is commensurate with those interests. Many existing systems of citizenship allocation lead to problems and anomalies: some people are left without citizenship through the accident of being born to non-citizen parents in a *ius sanguinis* regime; others grow up from infancy in a *ius soli* jurisdiction and find it hard to regularize their status.

While some people lack access to membership and suffer all kinds of legal and practical disabilities as a result, others, through accident of ancestry and birth, manage to acquire multiple citizenships. Different countries have different regimes and different laws on matters such as dual citizenship, giving many people an uncomfortable choice between protecting their effective rights in their place of residence and losing rights in their country of origin. In addition, many people who work transnationally, such as temporary migrant workers, have interests that are not best addressed simply by giving them membership in their particular place of residence.

A just global membership regime would therefore harmonize principles of membership acquisition via some convention on the subject as well as finding solutions for representing the interests of transnational workers. Some principle of membership such as Joseph Carens's social membership theory might form the basis for part of such a convention, but the important thing is for everyone's interests to be effectively included somewhere.

Third, if international mobility is to be a realistic and not merely a formal possibility, and if co-operative institutions for welfare and health are to be sustained, states have to develop ways in which entitlements built up at one location can be accessed effectively at another location, since the alternative to this is that those who choose to move in later life either become a burden on their new society or are left with inadequate protection, neither of which is a happy outcome. The way in which the European Union combines freedom of movement with access to healthcare across different jurisdictions could be one model for this, although as with many things, the sheer inequalities in wealth that exist across the planet would be a significant barrier.

Some arguments for limits

In principle, what reasons might count in a deliberation concerning whether the right to freedom of movement could be outweighed by some other interest or value? I have already mentioned environmental concerns, so I will not discuss them further. Four other areas strike me as plausible areas where some restriction might be justified: these involve (a) questions of cultural identity; (b) questions of collective autonomy and self-government; (c) questions involving the operation and integrity of co-operative institutions such as welfare states and health provision; (d) questions involving the loss of human capital through so-called 'brain drain'. The first three of these concern problems arising from inward migration to a state and the last, unusually, concerns the issue of emigration.

Cultural integrity

Concerns about the effect of immigration on cultural identity are often raised by populations of wealthy states who worry about whether the character of their state or town will change as a result of incomers from a different ethnic, linguistic or religious background. Such concerns can sometimes be the form in which straightforwardly racist attitudes get presented in the public forum, but in principle there seems to be nothing wrong with a desire that one's cultural environment remain relatively stable. But in a liberal society, the fact that someone, even many people, have strong desires that their form of life remain unchanged, is not necessarily a legitimate reason for enlisting the power of the state in its support.

Just as a resident's strong preference that most of the people in her street share her ethno-cultural background does not give her legitimate grounds for blocking the sale of houses to members of minorities, a strong desire that there be fewer foreigners settle in the country on the grounds of its ethnic or cultural character falls short of an acceptable reason to use state power against them. There is also a paradox of numbers involved: a very small number of foreign settlers does not change the cultural character of an area and, to the extent that it does, is likely to do so in ways welcomed by many natives; when numbers are larger and immigrants and their descendants are full members of a society, then there are no acceptable liberal grounds for favouring one set of cultural norms over another. Even where we can adduce neutral justifications for limiting cultural change, such as the need to keep transactional costs down, the interest in doing so would have to outweigh the interests the immigrants have in moving and settling, which may be considerable if they include economic opportunities, escaping persecution or maintaining family ties.

Which is not to say that there could be no such cases. Imagine, for example, a small island paradise inhabited by members of a distinctive culture who earn little more than a subsistence living by some fishing and a little agriculture. This is a way of life that the vast majority of them value and wish to continue and they have no desire for significantly increased wealth. However, the island is much prized as a tourist destination by wealthy Americans, some of whom have started to buy up land to build second or third homes for their retirement. The wealthy Americans have an interest in migration and settlement, but it is a weak one because they can easily satisfy their most vital interests elsewhere and because there is a wide range of alternative island paradises on which to construct homes. In the circumstances described, I can imagine the interest the islanders have in their local environment being sufficiently strong to outweigh the claim that the wealthy Americans have to settle.

Wellman's self-determination argument

One highly-influential argument for the right of states to regulate migration has been provided by the philosopher Christopher Heath Wellman. Wellman argues that legitimate states have this right because they have a right to self-determination that includes a right of freedom of association. Specifically, he thinks the right to exclude follows from three premises:

1. Legitimate states are entitled to self-determination,
2. Freedom of association is an integral component of self-determination, and
3. Freedom of association entitles one not to associate with others.

He concludes from this that 'legitimate states may choose not to associate with foreigners, including potential immigrants, as they see fit.'[12]

Wellman's argument is, on the face of things, highly persuasive and, as he points out, is consonant with our intuitions about some other cases. For instance, one example of the right to freedom of association is the right to marry. The right to marry gives people the option of choosing to spend their life with someone, but also includes the right to decline suitors. It does not imply a duty to marry, and while it is unfortunate if someone wishes to marry but cannot find anyone to marry them, it is not an injustice that cries out for correction. Wellman also draws out a number of other analogies, with companies, clubs and other private associations that have the right to admit people to membership, but also the discretion to exclude people who want to join: it is up to them.

However, on closer inspection, Wellman's argument looks problematic. Take the first premise: the right to self-determination only applies to what he calls legitimate states. A lot is going to depend on what it takes for a state to count as legitimate. Wellman's view is that a state is legitimate 'only if it adequately protects the human rights of its constituents and respects the rights of all others.'[13] If we take a stringent view of what is necessary adequately to protect and respect human rights, it may turn out that very few actual states (or even none) pass the threshold needed to secure legitimacy. The United States, with its brutal law-enforcement and prison regime and its carelessness for the lives of foreign civilians during its many wars, might not count as legitimate. The many states that act to prevent refugees finding sanctuary could likewise fail the test of legitimacy. José Jorge Mendoza has argued that the practice of immigration enforcement inevitably leads to human rights violations such that no state seeking to restrict immigration could do so while also achieving the moral legitimacy necessary for it to have the right to do so on Wellman's theory, suggesting a fatal paradox at the heart of his view.[14]

Parallels with marriage and private associations also look difficult to sustain. States, unlike marriages and private clubs, are not, for the most part, voluntary associations that people choose to join, but, rather compulsory coercive bodies that nearly everyone gets membership of because of their birth. In fact, states structure both the family and private associations through law, in order to protect justice and the rights of individuals. A marriage, as a legal institution, can only be entered into and dissolved according to certain public criteria that have changed markedly over time: states have often prevented some people from marrying one another through laws on the gender, age or number of their potential partners, and have insisted that separation be accompanied by a fair division of the marital assets and the security of the interests of any children. In many jurisdictions the freedom of association of clubs and other private bodies is limited by anti-discrimination laws to prevent them from excluding people on the basis of gender or race. Far from supporting a discretionary right to exclude, then, these allegedly parallel cases suggest that rights to exclude need to be at least qualified by concerns for justice and for the interests of all the people affected.

Wellman's focus on freedom of association as the basis for a right to exclude immigrants also creates an awkward tension between individual and collective freedom of association. A democratic decision by the people of a legitimate state to clamp down on immigration inevitably means that individuals who are citizens of that state are prevented from (or face grave difficulties in) associating with non-citizens for economic, cultural, romantic and many other reasons. Wellman's paradigm example, marriage, is an area where the assertion of states' rights of exclusion has meant that many people have been separated from their partners and children. While both individual and collective rights to freedom of association seem of great moral importance, Wellman's approach leads to the collective right always taking precedence over the individual right, and this seems implausible.

Wellman's argument does, however, have the interesting feature that it purports to block some justice- and rights-based arguments for freedom of movement across borders. Arguments that states must admit outsiders because those outsiders are unjustly excluded from some share of wealth or opportunity, or that states are under a duty to admit refugees on human rights grounds can be undercut just so long as there is something else that a state that wishes to exclude is able and willing to do to meet those claims. So if a person in a poor country is unable to enjoy a share of wealth and income to which she is entitled or is unjustly prevented from exploring valuable opportunities by border controls, an alternative to lifting those controls is to take steps to ensure that the person's just claims are met in their country of origin. Similarly, a legitimate state's duties to refugees can be met by securing adequate sanctuary for the refugee somewhere, which need not involve admitting the refugee to the territory of the state but might, rather, take the form of paying some other state to provide asylum.

These arguments are conditional in form. They preserve the legitimate state's supposed right to exclude just in case the state meets some condition. It is an empirical matter whether such a condition can be met. Wellman suggests that a state might meet its obligations of global distributive justice through foreign aid and, having met these obligations, would no longer be under a duty to admit poor foreigners. A lot is going to hang on the details. If a state provides foreign aid but this foreign aid is ineffective in securing real improvements in the lives of people in the target country, it will look as if their reasons to migrate to a wealthier one are undiminished, and much foreign aid is ineffective. If foreign aid seems likely to improve the circumstances of future generations, would a state that gave it thereby immunize itself from the claims of a member of the present generation to immigrate? And does the provision of aid to one country count as doing enough globally to secure a state against the claims of poor people from a different one?

The most important difficulty with Wellman's position, though, is that he purports to demonstrate more than he actually does, even for his ideal case of the legitimate state. Values such as the right to self-determination and the right to freedom of association are important, but they have to find their place among other significant values. Wellman makes some space for this by arguing that legitimate states can cater for some of those other values, such as distributive justice and human rights protection, in other ways, and he may be partially successful for the ideal case. Self-determination and freedom of association are often, however, values that can be catered to or satisfied to a greater or lesser degree. Large cities, such as New York or London, can exercise the collective self-determination of their inhabitants to quite a large extent even though they lack the capacity to exclude would-be immigrants. There may be levels of migration that would overwhelm a community's capacity for self-determination but this hardly entails a unilateral right to restrict immigration at any level, nor even a right to assert what the threatening level is. Self-determination is a valuable goal to be promoted among others rather than a value that always grounds a veto power.

Worries about the welfare state

One effect of immigration is that residents and taxpayers of a territory become exposed to positive duties of assistance that they never agreed to. If immigrants cross the border to live on the territory, existing residents will have to pay more to help them if they become sick or destitute. Even if costs are bearable, services need planning and organizing, and the unanticipated arrival of immigrants makes this harder. David Miller has argued that states need control over migration to limit their exposure to costs and to allow them to make meaningful plans.[15] This argument seems overstated. Many institutions, from town councils, to universities, to corporations, make plans without knowing the future conditions they will face, some of which are outside of their control. The fact that they could plan better if they had control over those conditions falls short of an argument that they are morally entitled to such control. Universities, for example, face future uncertainties because citizens may choose to have larger or smaller families or because governments have tighter or laxer controls on overseas students. They have to plan regardless, factoring in estimates of future uncertainty.

Miller also argues that the welfare state, and perhaps institutions of distributive justice more generally, require us to place limits on immigration, because such institutions require a degree of social trust that is harder to achieve in culturally hetero-geneous societies. He worries that societies that are divided into culturally separate segments will find it difficult to agree upon and operate policies that look to the common interest, because people will no longer identify with the entire national body but rather with their sub-group and that the policy process will be transformed into one of suspicious and self-interested group bargaining, where each cultural group sees a gain to others as a loss to itself and monitors whether it is a net beneficiary of, or contributor to, the country's tax-and-spend.

The argument amounts to saying that insiders have a right to exclude outsiders because, were they not to do so, they would end up being less just or generous to one another. But it is hard to see why this is a convincing argument when addressed to the excluded outsider: what reason has she to accept it, when it makes no reference to her interests whatsoever? Perhaps there are versions of the argument that are less vulnerable to this objection. After all, restrictions have to be justifiable to everyone, and perhaps there are circumstances where poor insiders would do so badly under a more open migration policy that they have a right to object. But if the reason that the poor insiders are doing badly is because of the indifferent and unjust attitudes of the wealthiest in their society, it is hard to see that the remedy for this is the coercive exclusion of foreigners rather than getting their compatriots to live up to their obligations.

There is another reason why arguments based on the welfare state are problematic. Welfare states come in significantly different types. Some welfare states distribute many benefits on the basis of membership, need, or even territorial presence alone. Others are more squarely based on a contributory or insurance principle according to which entitlement to benefits is dependent on having already made payments into the scheme. Probably no welfare state is purely of the contributory or non-contributory type. Some services, such as emergency medicine for people involved in car accidents, need to be available to anyone who is present on the territory, whether they have contributed in the past or not. Non-contributory schemes may commend themselves to taxpayers because the cost of treating people who have never paid taxes is more than offset by saving the administrative costs of operating a complicated insurance scheme. The central point here, though, is that the objection that immigration makes co-operative schemes run by the state vulnerable to unforeseen costs loses some force when we realize that it is possible to run schemes that exclude non-contributors from many, though not all, of their benefits. This would not be so, if there were some requirement of justice obliging us to choose the non-contributory variant over the contributory one, but it is hard to see that this is so for many welfare benefits.

These concerns about planning, cost and state functions are not entirely without merit, but they do not prove as much as they claim. Other social processes that result from individual choice expose state functions to similar potential costs and uncertainties. But we often judge that protecting people's freedom to make some choices that have disruptive effects is sufficiently important that we should live with the consequences. For example, if we want to preserve reproductive choices for families, then we run the risk that they end up having more children than anticipated and thereby impose costs and adjustments on school systems or health services and strains on the environment. (Sometimes the problem is that our plans are undermined when people have too few children.) Similarly, if we are trying to think about a set of principles to regulate global migration, then it would seem excessive to allow states unilateral discretion to close their borders simply on the hypothetical worry that their internal systems might be subjected to unanticipated strains. Doing so would give the interests of members in running their co-operative arrangements smoothly an absolute priority over the interests that would-be immigrants have in coming to settle on the territory.

There is every reason why the interests of members in things like welfare services should count when we look at what is justifiable to everyone; there is no reason why they should outweigh other, potentially more urgent reasons. There is a general presumption that people should not be judges in their own case, and a similar reasoning should apply here. In the case where some state wanted to restrict migration because of the strain on its co-operative arrangements – something that was occasionally mooted for EU migration in the case of the UK under the name of an 'emergency brake' – then it is reasonable that it be expected to provide evidence of specific harms and that the costs and benefits be assessed by an impartial third party, rather than simply giving a state discretion to exclude.

Brain drain

International human rights law recognizes a right of exit from countries. Generally speaking, states may not compel their citizens to remain within their borders and may not prevent them from seeking a life elsewhere. But some people worry that permitting people to leave their countries can have negative consequences for those they leave behind, can tend to skew the income distribution in poorer states towards greater inequality, and can disincentivize states from investing in training skilled people, such as doctors and nurses. It is fair to say that the economic findings on so-called 'brain drain' are mixed, with many economists arguing that countervailing factors, including the development of skills by those hoping to work abroad, the later return of skilled professionals and the remittances they send back home, more than outweigh any negative effects on poor societies.[16] Still, in deciding what an ideally just migration regime would look like, we need to decide whether we should factor in possible harms caused by talented people who leave poor countries, and whether these could justify more restrictive policies.

If a talented person leaves a poor country, and some people there are worse off as a result, we cannot conclude that those people have been harmed. This is because doing something which leaves a person worse off than they otherwise would be is not sufficient to harm them. If I could give my last mint to Alan or Beryl and choose to give it to Alan, I do not harm Beryl, even though Beryl is worse off as a result of my choice than she otherwise would be. If I am entitled to act in a certain way, and there is nobody who has a right that I act otherwise, then my action will not count as an unjust harm to them. To have grounds to *make* someone act in a certain way, by, for example, preventing them from leaving the country, we have to establish that they are under a morally enforceable duty.[17] But establishing this is hard.

Philosophers typically distinguish between the general duties that people have to others and the special duties that arise because they are in some relationship with others or have made an agreement with others. They also distinguish between positive duties (roughly, duties to help, including duties of rescue) and negative duties (duties not to harm). General duties, such as the negative duty not to punch people on the nose and the positive duty to save a child from drowning, fall on all of us, independently of the relationships in which we stand to those people. But we may have special duties towards others because we are a parent of a child, a fellow citizen, or because we have made an agreement with them.

The most plausible non-contractual claim that talented people are under a duty not to leave their country of origin would be that they have a special duty towards their least advantaged fellow citizens not to do so. It seems likely that we are under some special duties if we live in a reasonably just and legitimate state and partake of institutions that provide valuable public goods or other services such as medical care. For example, I may have a duty to pay my taxes and not to evade them. But the claim that I have a duty not to leave is stronger than this: it does not simply say that I am under a duty to contribute to a co-operative scheme in which I am a participant, but also that I must continue to contribute to that scheme. It also says that such a duty of continued participation is sufficiently strong to outweigh other considerations, such as my right to pursue my own plans and projects as I see fit and competing duties I might have, such as to family members or co-religionists, which might point to emigration.

Where states provide valuable training on reasonable terms to people who are old enough to consent to those terms, things may be a little different. There may seem to be nothing objectionable in principle to states saying to people who want to be doctors or nurses that a condition of their state-funded training is that they either commit to service within the country for some limited period or repay the cost of their training. Even here, though, some qualifications apply. If the state is a monopoly supplier of training or the only realistic funder of such training by others, then it should not abuse its position by making such terms too onerous. On the face of it, requiring that people who have voluntarily contracted to do so spend three or four years working in a location in need of medical professionals seems well within the range of what is reasonable.

We should, though, notice the limited nature of what is being claimed here. First, the obligation is a contractual one rather than one that applies to a person as a citizen of a community: a foreign national trained within the same system could be subject to the same obligations. Second, the fact that the contract is with the state is merely a contingent part of the picture: a non-state provider of medical services and training could offer a similar deal. Third, training that the state offers in return for an offer of service or repayment has to be training that it was not under an obligation to provide to its citizens pursuant to its duties to secure them reasonable and equal opportunities in life. In other words, the state may not place conditions on the provision of opportunities that it is under an obligation to provide unconditionally. I conclude, therefore, that 'brain drain', if it is indeed a real phenomenon, provides little basis for limiting rights of emigration and that any such constraints that are justified are, in fact, voluntary contractual restraints that apply in a few circumstances only.

Conclusion

The most important feature of a just global migration regime is that it is procedural rather than substantive. That is to say, that it should be a system according to which claims of right and duty bearing on people moving from one location to live or to work at another, particularly claims to exclude, should be adjudicated in a way that is in principle justifiable to everyone rather than being the unilateral imposition on some by others. Doing this in practice would involve two things: first, a global convention covering the basic principles at stake, and second, some institutional machinery for operating and interpreting those principles and for resolving disagreements. Obviously, that procedural machinery does not currently exist and is merely aspirational.

Substantively, such a regime would contain a strong presumption in favour of freedom of movement, but the reasons that many philosophers and political theorists have adduced in favour of restrictions on mobility would not be silent. Rather, they would count among reasons that could in principle support a claim to restrict, where they were sufficiently weighty. The important thing about such claims is that they would need to be vindicated in terms of reasons that apply to everyone and could no longer simply be something that members of states imposed unilaterally on outsiders.

Readers may be thinking at this point that this plan for global co-operation around migration is rather utopian and of dubious relevance to our present condition. The next chapter aims to address this worry. Given that we do not live in a world regulated from a common perspective but rather in the actual world of supposedly sovereign states who are somewhat reined in by international law, what implications does the idea of a future justified regime have for the conduct of states, and, for that matter, of individuals?

3

Obligations of Individuals and States in an Unjust World

A global migration regime with a presumption in favour of free movement might sound like a nice idea, giving individuals the opportunity to escape more easily from poverty or oppression, freeing us from the intrusive scrutiny of border officials, and allowing us to explore a range of economic, cultural, religious or romantic opportunities much greater than those available in the particular country where we were born. But an obvious objection presents itself. A world like that might be a better world than the one we presently live in, and it might be a more just world, but there is a considerable distance between it and the one in which we now live. Given there is no global system for the regulation of migration of the type that justice requires, where does that leave us?

In this chapter I first ask what the responsibilities

of individuals in such an unjust world are. Second, I look at what states may do to put themselves in better standing in circumstances where other states remain determined to act unjustly. The two are clearly linked. Where individuals are members of states, one thing they should do is to work towards the improvement of their state's laws and policies; in order to do that they need some idea of what is possible and desirable in the world as it actually is.

Duties of individuals

A world in which states simply assert their right to unilaterally exclude would-be migrants, and where they refuse to work to create a just global migration regime is a world in which a kind of tyranny is imposed upon the excluded. It is a world in which people have their freedom limited by state power unjustly wielded against them. Such unilateral exclusion also severely limits their life-opportunities and can lock them into societies where they are permanently disadvantaged. Where states have agreed to provide asylum for victims of persecution we have seen how they often make it as difficult as possible for those refugees to assert their rights, and how they knowingly expose those fleeing persecution to risks of serious injury, even death. The world in which states, and particularly wealthy states, pursue the unilateral exclusionary policies that they do is a world of serious injustice, with those policies among the things that makes it so.

The question therefore arises of what obligations individuals possess in such a world. Two sorts of individuals are particularly relevant here: first, the migrants themselves; and second, the citizens of states that are unjustly pursuing exclusionary policies. However, we need to be wary of treating these as mutually exclusive categories. As we saw in chapter 1, there are many citizens who are themselves immigrants or of immigrant origin; or whose interests are deeply intertwined with migrant friends, family and colleagues; many other people who are present on the territory who don't fit the ideal model of citizen neatly, and others who are disadvantaged because their race or ethnic origin is similar to that of migrants.

For both migrants and citizens of excluding states, it will often be sensible and prudent to try to comply with immigration law. The simple reason for this is that there is a vast imbalance of force between states and individuals. States have formidable capacity to detect and punish non-compliance and often hold non-compliance against individuals for a very long time, perhaps even for life. Moreover, states will often structure the practices they regulate so that non-compliance is effectively impossible: in many jurisdictions, a large institution, such as a university or a hospital, simply could not succeed in employing a lecturer or doctor without the legal right to work in the country. My focus here is not, however, on what it is prudent to do, but on what people are morally required or permitted to do.

Among the class of migrants, it is irregular migrants, that is, those without state authorization, who are the most obvious victims of exclusionary policies. This group may include poor economic migrants, but may also contain refugees whom the state is preventing from accessing the territory. Unauthorized migrants are often subject to accusations, both by politicians and by ordinary citizens, that they are lawbreakers who are worthy of exclusion, detention or punishment. But as we have seen, irregular migrants are hardly the only group who suffer from unjust or capricious policies. For example, even those migrants who are legally present on the territory are often rendered vulnerable to exploitation and abuse by measures such as restrictive visa conditions. Others, separated from friends and relations by family visa rules, are also among the victims. Where migrants engage in deception to evade immigration rules or restrictions on their right to work, politicians and the media often represent this as a mark against the migrants' moral character that further demonstrates their unworthiness for admission. And when migrants damage property or use some degree of force to evade controls, this is often taken as further evidence of their criminality or unsuitability.

In the actual world, migrants, both authorized and unauthorized, engage in a great deal of non-compliance with immigration laws and border controls. When states put measures in place such as walls, carrier sanctions and visa restrictions, some immigrants will try to enter the territory by other means; perhaps taking dangerous journeys by boat, deceiving government officials by providing false information or producing forged documents, or entering a 'marriage of convenience'. Some non-compliance will be low-level, as when people fail to act in accordance with the terms of a visa by, say, working when they are not supposed to. At the opposite extreme, someone might engage in deliberate violence against physical infrastructure by destroying a perimeter fence, or against border officers or law enforcement, in order to gain entry or to remain on the territory. And though some non-compliance is deliberate, quite a lot is unwitting, because states are prone to change the often Byzantine rules so as to render what was previously legal illegal.

How much, if any, of this non-compliance is justifiable in relation to states that are acting unjustly? From the would-be immigrant's point of view, such states are engaged in unilateral coercion against them, attempting to limit their freedom and determine their actions through force or the threat of force. Such unilateral coercion may or may not be a threat to the migrant's vital interests, but where it is, then the migrant's right to self-defence comes into play; assuming, as most people believe, that individuals have the right to use self-defence against threats to their life and vital interests. Within a state, an individual's right to self-defence is usually somewhat limited by the existence of police and courts that can come to a person's aid against an aggressor, so that the claims of necessity apply to a reduced range of cases. But public law enforcement agencies, accountable to all citizens and impartial among them, are often not available in the same way to irregular migrants, and such agencies are often in the position of being unjustified aggressors themselves.[1]

We cannot infer from this that 'anything goes' on

the part of the migrant. All individuals have general moral duties that hold outside of any association or relationship in which they find themselves. Would-be migrants whose vital interests are at stake may have a right to use reasonable force against state agents in self-defence, but any such force must be both proportionate and necessary. And the refugee or the person fleeing extreme poverty who needs to use force to evade border guards and make it onto the territory is in a very different position to a comparatively well-off would-be migrant whose options outside the territory are more satisfactory.

The permissibility of deception is already recognized in international law in situations where refugees need to get past borders to escape persecution. Where unjustly excluded migrants can only access or remain on the territory by deception, I take it that they may do so. The same goes if they need to use false documents or similar means in order to work, find somewhere to live, or access vital services. Engaging in such deception is a way of thwarting the plans of people or institutions who aim unjustly to limit their freedom, and this seems entirely permissible when it is necessary for people to protect their vital interests.

Citizens of excluding states, at least where the society is democratic, are participants in the making of exclusionary laws. They are often also co-opted by the state to enforce those laws through 'hostile environment' policies that require them not to employ, shelter or assist irregular migrants. As ordinary members of society, they may have to decide whether to participate in exclusionary practices; but also whether to assist migrants in ways that might include sheltering them from immigration enforcement, providing transport or merely giving humanitarian assistance. As political agents, citizens may choose to use their votes for or against immigration laws, and may contest laws that they regard as unjust through protest, civil disobedience or other acts of resistance.

Often people think that citizens have a general duty to comply even with unjust laws, so long as they are not outrageously so. This might be because the country is a democracy and citizens have played a part in the process that decided these laws. Alternatively, it might be for reasons of justice. For example, people should normally pay the taxes that sustain co-operative institutions within their society even when it falls short of what a completely fair society would look like. The fact that such arrangements enable us to preserve our freedom, and to enjoy the benefits of co-operation with others, normally gives us strong reasons for compliance, especially when there are normal political means at our disposal to seek reform.

But there are powerful countervailing reasons in some cases. First, if the state is democratic, then the citizen shares responsibility for its unjust policies. Where the victims of those policies are non-members who have neither voice nor vote, democracy's legitimating force is reduced and citizens' responsibility not to be part of the commission of injustice gains increased salience. This responsibility may require them to protest against the injustice and perhaps to take some action to compensate the victims of the unjust policies. Second, some laws and policies are so egregiously unjust that nobody has an obligation to comply with them: for example, laws requiring racial discrimination or outlawing homosexuality. Immigration laws, by reinforcing global injustice, subjecting individuals to unilateral coercion and thwarting many in their most basic interests often involve very grave injustice. Moreover, the effects of immigration policies in undermining equality among citizens can give powerful reasons for resistance even in terms of domestic justice: a good example here is the way that 'hostile environment' policies make it more difficult for citizens from racial or ethnic minorities to find jobs or rent homes because they 'look like' immigrants.

Plausibly, citizens of democratic states with unjust immigration laws have three types of duty. First, they have a duty to work with other citizens to change the law and to get their own state and society to play its part in building and maintaining a just regulatory framework for migration. Some suggestions concerning what states must do are set out below, and conscientious citizens who recognize the injustice of existing migration law will work to move states and policy-makers to reduce or mitigate that injustice. Such work may take the form of political campaigning or protest, as well as engaging in civil disobedience and resistance against the most unjust laws and policies. It may also consist of working to inform a democratic public of the rights and wrongs of migration or providing resources for others to do so. Second, at least in many cases, they will have duties of non-compliance; at least where this is practically feasible and may be undertaken without excessive personal cost. So, for example, if doctors or teachers are able to effectively resist state directives to report on, or deny medical treatment or education to, irregular migrants, then they should. Third, they have duties directly to mitigate the worst effects of unjust migration policies on the victims of those policies. Such mitigation could take many forms. It could involve providing practical assistance to irregular migrants in the form of rescue, shelter or food, as many conscientious people have done in places such as the Greek islands or the Arizona desert. But it could also be discharged by providing financial support for NGOs and charities who provide such assistance.

Given the willingness of states to criminalize and punish the actions of those who assist irregular migrants, it may be excusable for individuals not to risk those punishments but to limit their actions to joining protests against injustice or to acting through normal political means. But while standing aside may be excusable in such circumstances, it is surely permissible and indeed laudable for ordinary citizens to assist the unjustly excluded even at the risk of such punishment; whether by giving them material and practical assistance, or by thwarting the state in its unjust enforcement efforts through failures to co-operate, deceiving and misdirecting its agents, and so forth.

Duties of states

The key defect I identified with the system of state discretionary control over migration was its unilateralism. States claim the right to subject outsiders to coercive exclusion in terms that cannot be justified from a perspective that those outsiders can share. That generates an imperative to create a regulatory system of some kind that can be justifiable to everyone. Still, it also leaves open the question of what states are bound to do and what states have permission to do in the here and now, when no such system yet exists. Do we declare all unilateral policies by states illegitimate? Or, at the opposite extreme, do we say that in the absence of a globally just regime, states may do as they like?

The argument for straightforward illegitimacy is the familiar one that unilateral coercion expresses might rather than right. The argument that states may do as they wish is that states that go it alone, in circumstances where other states do not, by introducing highly permissive migration regimes, thereby potentially expose themselves to an unfair share of the costs of global migration. A crude expression of this thought would be to invoke hypothetical cases where all wealthy liberal democracies but one closed their borders to the global poor, with the consequence that many people beat a path to the door of that sole remaining open country. Perhaps all states are under a duty to bring a just migration regime into being in co-operation with others, but in the absence of an assurance that those other states will also act, nobody, the thought goes, is under an obligation to do so alone. These stark alternatives are unsatisfactory.

Just as Kant's ideas about the unilateral imposition of duties were the inspiration for the critique of the regime of state discretionary choice, another Kantian idea offers a potential solution to this dilemma. Sometimes, Kant recognized, unilateral action is necessary for justice to gain a foothold. For example, in his theory of property, bringing about a regime where individual claims can be vindicated from a common perspective, might require some people to force others into a law-governed system. To think about cases such as this, Kant introduced the idea of 'permissive law', giving a moral excuse to actions necessary for the establishment of justice or, retrospectively, condoning those, such as the seizure of territory, where unwinding an earlier wrong threatens to undermine an existent system of justice.[2]

The important thing to keep in mind is that the right that individuals or states exercise under such 'permissive law' is both provisional and conditional. It is provisional pending the establishment of a proper system of authorization from everyone's perspective, and it is conditional on the right-holder working towards that establishment. Individuals and states cannot simply rest on their laurels and assert their rights against others unless they are actively working to end the imperfection of a condition where some inevitably force their will onto others.

What, then, should we require of a state in a world where many other states are not willing to submit themselves to a regime of just regulation? Plausibly three things: first, that they should actively work towards such a regime in co-operation with other states and actors; second, that they should unilaterally implement a border regime in their own case that is somewhat sensitive to the costs they would be exposed to in a world where everyone else was conforming to a just regime; and third, that they should respect the human rights that everybody has, but, in this context, particularly the human rights of migrants. States that fail to do these things, or so I shall argue, completely forfeit the rights to control which they claim for themselves and nobody – neither their citizens nor immigrants – is under a moral obligation to comply with their immigration policies. States that sincerely attempt to bring a just regime into being have some claims to expect compliance with their policies, though even here there are limits.

Duties of co-operation with others

The duties a state and its citizens have to co-operate with others to bring a regime of justice into being with respect to migration are part of a more general duty that they have in relation to the global order. Agreeing a framework of international law to govern things like natural resources and the law of the sea, as well as general human rights, are part of the same general project. What may be somewhat distinctive about migration is that a just regulatory regime cannot simply be a matter for states but also calls for the involvement of migrants themselves and indeed of the full range of 'people who don't fit' whom we have already encountered. States should work with these others to establish conventions and the institutional machinery for making them operate and to provide the resources necessary for this to happen. Some of this work is constructive: talking and acting to bring new institutional mechanisms into being. But some of it is also concerned with the maintenance of existing co-operative systems and standing up against attempts to undermine them.

For example, many states are signatories to the 1951 Refugee Convention and its later extension. The Convention is far from perfect, but it is an *acquis*, an improvement on what went before as well as a step towards a more just order. States that abide by the rules of the Convention, that seek to develop them in ways that extend protection in line with its founding spirit, that try to persuade new states to accept the Convention's obligations, and which work to support, develop or reform other features of the refugee regime, such as The Office of the United Nations High Commissioner for Refugees (UNHCR) are doing the minimum of what justice requires in this area. States which refuse to sign the Convention, or which, having signed, act to undermine its operation and weaken the effective protection refugees enjoy, as most wealthy states currently do, are not. Similarly, states that co-operate with one another and with global agencies to secure protections for temporary migrant workers or to harmonize citizenship laws so as to guard against statelessness are working in the right direction, and those who seek to undermine existing protections are doing the opposite.

Duties of fair shares

Are states who are committed to a just global migration regime required to open their own borders to the extent to which they would have to if that just regime were in place, given that other states unjustly refuse to? The worry, as we have seen, is that this exposes just states to an unfair share of costs that they would not have to bear under a fully just regime. One obvious line of thought to pursue in response to this risk is that states committed to justice must supply their fair share of what justice ideally requires but are not under a duty to compensate for the unjust non-compliance of others.

Although 'fair shares' seems superficially plausible, it is a view that comes with some acute problems. First of all, to the extent that excluding some migrants would involve harming them or otherwise violating their rights, it does not even seem relevant. My duty to refrain from doing such things to people does not seem like something that is conditional on the willingness or unwillingness of others also to refrain. Perhaps a more promising venue for a fair shares view is where state admission of migrants is similar to cases of rescue or assistance. Admission of refugees and other displaced persons can look like this when we think of it as the application of a humanitarian duty. Some philosophers have found a fair shares view attractive in thinking about humanitarian duties because doing so limits the sacrifices that individuals are obliged to make to help famine victims in distant countries to levels that don't look too demanding.[3] Where other citizens fail to do their bit to help, say, famine victims, the conscientious person is not obliged to

111

take up the slack but only to do their bit. But here, too, the implication that people can blamelessly abandon suffering victims as soon as they have done their 'share' looks unattractive, prioritizing as it does fairness among the rescuers above the acute claims of victims.[4]

In relation to refugees or the displaced victims of natural disasters, discussing the 'fair share' of wealthy countries also comes with a sense of unreality, since the main countries facing the burden of housing them today falls on poorer countries such as Turkey, Pakistan and Ethiopia rather than on the rich ones in Europe and North America. However, in theory we could think of some principles, perhaps incorporating variables such as a country's population, its usable land area or its per capita national income.[5] Even were we to come up with such a set of quotas in this way, however, no mechanical application of such a formula could tell the whole story, for the simple reason that we should also take account of the legitimate needs and wishes of displaced persons themselves, who may prefer to be close to family members, to be in a society that is culturally close to theirs, and to be able to make use of valuable skills, including languages they can speak.

Still, with these caveats in mind, we can see that

some notion of fair shares could play a role in distributing refugees among states and in inter-state arguments about who should do what. Where states are considering, for example, quotas of refugees and other displaced persons for resettlement from refugee camps or poor countries, they could be used to generate some numerical guidance. Such numbers could not be used, however, to justify a state in abandoning its commitment to the *non-refoulement* and assessment of individuals arriving on the territory. The function of such quotas would be to guide the rights and duties that states have against one another; they could not be used to deny sanctuary to individuals, though they could provide reasons for relocating individuals from one compliant state to another. The provision of safe routes for people to escape from situations of war and persecution and the abandonment of policies that force those escaping to take life-threatening journeys and to place themselves in the hands of criminal gangs are also necessary conditions for states to enjoy provisional good standing.

Fair shares works, then, imperfectly at best, and often not at all, when thinking about cases where individuals have an urgent claim to relocation on grounds such as refugee status or family attachment. Still, we might find a residual role for the idea in the following way: we might try to estimate the numbers of people who would migrate to particular countries under a just global migratory regime where exclusion would have to be justified to all, plausibly a regime of few restrictions, and then use this to think about a quota that a just state is obliged to fill anyway, given non-compliance. Many of the places in that quota would already be taken by those with a claim to priority, but this would leave a residue of places that would be available to others, perhaps via a random or lottery system. All members of the group of people with an in-principle claim to entry would be allocated a ticket, and those lucky enough to draw a winning ticket would be granted an entry visa.

Phillip Cole has plausibly argued that any such system would still be unfair and in violation of liberal principles and that any defence of it on the grounds that we need some kind of decision-making mechanism will fail because it could not secure the consent of all those subject to it.[6] This is very much in line with the central argument of the previous chapter, that a fully just system for the global regulation of migration has to be answerable to everyone it applies to. But the problem here concerns what states must do to put themselves in 'good standing' pending the establishment of a just global regime. It is hard to resist the idea that a lottery or something like it would be the fairest way of proceeding, however imperfect that might be by an absolute standard. Still, we might also think of ways in which states could reduce the legitimacy deficit by consulting with the wider population beyond their borders, as well as with recent immigrants, about the design and implementation of their allocation systems. This would fall far short of the ideal, but then we are addressing the characteristics of an explicitly transitional and only provisionally justified regime that is intermediate between unilateral discretionary control and a just global order.

I have considered problems that might arise for a state committed to justice in a world where other states were not, problems that arise from simple failures of other states to do their share. Still, it is possible to imagine worse scenarios. In a world with a lot of free movement, unjust states might actively try to offload parts of their population onto other states.[7] These might include people too old or sick to work, who nevertheless cost a lot to look after, or they might include members of unwanted ethnic minorities such as Myanmar's Rohingya displaced to India or Bangladesh, or they might be settlers from a predatory state looking to increase the numbers of their group on the territory of a neighbouring state as part of a project of forcible annexation.[8] In some of these cases, a provisionally legitimate state, otherwise working sincerely to bring a just global migration regime into being, would be entitled to refuse and exclude these new arrivals. In others, such as in cases involving 'ethnic cleansing', doing so would involve a failure of humanitarian duty towards individuals, and other methods, beginning with diplomatic pressures, would have to be used.

Duties to respect human rights

Even if we agree that a state operating within an international environment where other states are not willing to play their part in bringing a just global system into being has a provisional entitlement to control numbers, there will be strict limits on the means that it can employ to do so. As we have seen already, existing states employ methods to control their borders that systematically expose would-be immigrants to acute risks, which lead to many foreseeable and preventable deaths, and which rely on shady deals with undemocratic and illiberal states to restrict the movement of people across their territory. At the border, guards often employ violent methods to subdue those they believe have crossed illegally. Nor is this the end of the matter; states subject people they wish to classify as 'illegal' to detention in what are prisons in all but name, they deny people access to justice and impede their rights of appeal. By putting in place a hostile environment on the territory to deter migrants by making it impossible for them to access work, housing or basic health services, they both subject those people to acute deprivation but also often undermine equalities among their existing citizens. And bureaucracies in charge of detaining and removing those they have deemed 'illegal' often come to regard the human rights of those they control and their families not as a supreme value to be promoted and respected but rather as a series of technical, legal obstacles to policy to be circumvented whenever possible. It seems superfluous to extend further this list of charges because they are so widely known, at least among those interested in the subject of immigration if not, sadly, among the wider public.

A provisionally just regime seeking to operate an immigration policy with the aid of controlling numbers would have to eschew the use of methods which breach the human rights of immigrants and their families directly, which make it impossible to protect their general human rights against others, or which undermine the equal status of their own citizens. It is an open question how far this is possible.[9]

A state whose agents episodically breached human rights constraints, and who were subject to disciplinary action when they did so, would probably not forfeit its legitimate authority in the area. A state which knowingly engaged in or ignored such things would lack a right to exclude.

Conclusion

This chapter has argued for the view that states that are genuinely committed to introducing a just system to regulate global migration would be entitled to engage in some exclusionary policies. But it is important to note that this is an extremely minimal and transitional concession in the actual world where states, their politicians and electorates believe that they have an almost unlimited discretionary right to exclude foreigners; where human rights laws are seen as unfortunate obstacles to the 'popular will'. States in the actual world typically act with manifest injustice towards unwanted outsiders and casually expose them to violence, incarceration, risks of death and serious harm, exploitation and subordination. Such states may, in the best case, have a limited claim on the allegiance of their own citizens with respect to the legal and social systems that make life within the territory bearable, but they have no claim that either would-be immigrants or their own citizens must comply with their demands where those demands are manifestly unjust. Sometimes, of course, we have to do as we are told, because prudence is a better option than pointless martyrdom. But our attitude towards the injustice of states in the area of migration should be one of grudging acceptance at most. Neither immigrants nor citizens should accept that they have a duty to obey such laws.

Concluding Thoughts

Migration and mobility have always been a feature of human life and they always will be. People want to move for familiar reasons, including taking advantage of economic opportunities, to be with friends and family, and escaping from poverty or persecution. Some of these reasons for migration would be lessened in a more equal world than we have today or in one where everyone's human rights were respected. But others would not. In any event, migration, authorized or unauthorized, 'legal' or 'illegal', will continue to be a feature of our world and to shape our lives and societies.

It is foreseeable, too, that in democratic societies riven by anxieties about the future, both economic and cultural, there will be strong pressure from electorates to control migration and that politicians will often bend to such pressure either because they will gain advantage from doing so or because they, too, believe the same things as their voters. Where politicians take the opposite view and are more friendly to immigrants, they will often be keen to make sure that the incomers are of the 'right sort' and will have the skills to contribute to the economy or be of an age to make good demographic imbalances.

Even within particular states we have seen that the desire of countries to control migration, often under democratic pressure, can have terrible consequences for the liberal, democratic and egalitarian character of those societies, because of the presence on the territory of people who do not fit neatly into the container model of nation states and their citizens. Often those people are subjected to state power without having the right or opportunity to shape law and policy. Additionally, both the rule of law and the supposed equality of all before it are subverted by the unequal treatment that foreigners and even citizens who look like them experience.

The lesson of this book has been that we cannot think about the rights and wrongs of migration simply from the perspective of what is in the interest of the electorates of particular states. States are coercive institutions that restrict the freedom of individuals, but the standard justification for this is that they thereby make people better off, both in terms of their freedom and their well-being, compared to the alternative. This line of justification, though, is only plausible when those subjected to state power and its beneficiaries are the same people, an assumption that ceases to hold when we look beyond state borders and at the people who want to cross them.

The basis of the current regime governing international migration is that sovereign states have the right to control their borders and admit or refuse whoever they choose. I have rejected that norm because it involves some people coercing other people in ways that cannot be justified, an application of force rather than justice. It does not follow automatically that no borders or open borders is the right answer. Rather, any norms that govern international migration need to pass a test, a test of justifiability to everyone subject to them. That is hard for coercive border regimes to do when they lock people into poverty, stop them moving to get away from ecological catastrophe, trap them with their persecutors, separate them from their friends and split up their families. Measures with those kinds of effects need powerful reasons behind them. On our crowded and polluted planet we cannot exclude the possibility that sometimes there will be such reasons, but where they are in play, they need to be adjudicated in a way that is fair to everyone. A just migration regime will plausibly be one with very few coercive restrictions on human mobility.

Notes

Chapter 1: Migration Today and in History

1 All the figures here are taken from the *2015 Global Migration Trends Factsheet* (International Organization for Migration, 2015). Our knowledge of migration numbers is highly imperfect and much of it is produced by agencies based in countries that do not have the administrative systems in place and the resources to answer questions that they are interested in, so necessarily there is much we do not know.

2 Statistics from Vera Cohn and Rich Morin, 'American Mobility: Movers, Stayers, Places and Reasons', Pew Research Center. Cited in Huemer (2010), p. 451.

3 'Foreign citizens living in the EU Member States', eurostat newsrelease 230/2015, 18 December 2015.

4 For a discussion of this dynamic, see Mann (2011), chapter 3.

5 See Judt (2011), pp. 333–7 for a summary of the European experience.

6 See chapter 2 in Joppke (1999) on the impact of the 1965 Act.

7 As is very much the theme of Scott (2009).

8 For discussion of the ethnic homogenization of Europe, see Judt (2011), ch. 1.

9 Some writers have termed this kind of thinking 'methodological nationalism', an approach that systematically conflates 'society' with the 'nation state'. See Sager (2016a), pp. 229–30. See also Sager (2016b) and Dumitru (2014).

10 See Jones (2016), pp. 56–61.

11 See Abrahamian (2015) for discussion of this group.

12 For discussion, see Branko Milanovic on the 'citizen-ship rent', in Milanovic (2016), pp. 132–43.

13 See Carens (1987) and Shachar (2009).

14 See, for example, Easterly (2001).

15 The classic discussion of this is in Walzer (1983), pp. 46–8. For critical commentary, see Carens (2013), chapter 9.

16 The classic study documenting this particular bias in detail is Wray (2011).

17 In the UK, revisions of the citizenship law have meant that children born in the country to immigrant parents who have lived nowhere else can suddenly find in adulthood that their belief they were of British nationality is unfounded and can be threatened with removal from the country and deprived of the right to work. For example, see this report by Emily Dugan, 'This Woman Always Thought She Was British. Now, After 30 Years, The Home Office Says She's Not'. https://www.buzzfeed.com/emilydugan/

this-woman-always-thought-she-was-british-now-aft
er-30

18 See Lenard (2010).
19 Carens (2013).
20 Ottonelli and Torresi (2010). See also Owen
   (2013).
21 See Paul Mason, 'It's not enough to let EU residents
   stay – they should get the vote, too', *Guardian*, 26
   June 2017. https://www.theguardian.com/politics/co
   mmentisfree/2017/jun/26/eu-residents-vote-non-citiz
   ens-taxes
22 Good surveys of these developments are Jones (2016)
   and Andersson (2014).
23 For a wider exploration of this point, see Anderson
   (2013).
24 For shocking and incisive commentary on the 'foreign
   criminal' panic in the UK, see Griffiths (2017). See
   Prabhat (2017) for the political context to citizenship
   deprivation in the UK and for some of the normative
   issues.
25 See Carens (2013), chapter 7.
26 A theme explored in Sager (2017).
27 Arendt (1958), p. 296.
28 See Hathaway and Foster (2014), p. 17.

Chapter 2: Justifying a Migration Regime
from an Impartial Perspective

1 For discussion, see Morris (1998), chapter 2.
2 The best-known example that makes this assumption
  explicit is Rawls's (1971) closed society assumption.

3 A point rather vividly set out in the opening chapter of Huemer (2013).

4 Here I summarize some of Kant's approach as set out in Kant (1996a). I make no pretence at Kant scholarship here, though. My understanding owes much to Ripstein (2009).

5 Kant himself failed to draw this conclusion, and the line of thought I pursue here is 'Kantian' in inspiration rather than purporting to represent his thinking. Some scholars have found in his writings on 'cosmopolitan right' in Kant (1996b) the outlines of a normative theory of immigration that anticipates or endorses what I have called the 'container model'.

6 This was very much the theoretical approach of the French revolutionary Anacharsis Cloots, as explored in Kleingeld (2012), chapter 2.

7 In Rawls (1971).

8 Carens (1987).

9 For the complete list as Nussbaum sets it out, see Nussbaum (2000), pp. 77–80.

10 This is essentially the view advocated in Rawls (1993).

11 Depending on how stringent the requirements of democratic legitimacy are, this may be a difference between my approach and that of Abizadeh (2008).

12 From Wellman and Cole (2011), p. 13. See also Wellman (2008).

13 Wellman and Cole (2011), p. 16.

14 Mendoza (2015).

15 See Miller (2016), chapter 4. This form of argument can be extended to take account of other impacts

Notes to pp. 88–112

that immigration might have on the ability of states to perform their duties. So, for example, David Miller argues that states who have agreed to limit their carbon emissions might need to set a population target to do so and that this could be undermined by immigrants crossing open borders.

16 In 2015 financial remittances sent to origin countries by international migrants totalled USD581 billion, 75 per cent of which was sent to low- and middle-income countries. Remittance inflows for such countries are approximately three times more than the foreign aid they receive (International Organization for Migration, 2015).

17 For discussion of the problems with counterfactual conceptions of harm, see Holtug (2002) and Bradley (2012).

Chapter 3: Obligations of Individuals and States in an Unjust World

1 I am much influenced in this section by Hidalgo (2015).

2 My understanding of Kant's idea of permissive law comes from Ypi (2012) and from Roff (2013), chapter 3. Kant discusses the idea in Kant (1996b).

3 Fair shares is roughly the view defended in Murphy (2000).

4 A point made by Zofia Stemplowska in Stemplowska (2016).

5 For more extensive discussion of some of the issues

of fairness among states arising from obligations to refugees, see Gibney (2015).

6 Cole (2000), pp. 148–54.

7 Joseph Heath discusses the 'social dumping' scenario in Heath (1997).

8 I have heard people articulate the predatory settlement scenario as a worry for the Baltic states, for example.

9 For arguments that it is all but impossible to regulate migration without such impermissible actions, see Mendoza (2015) and Sager (2017).

References

Abizadeh, A. 2008. 'Democratic Theory and Border Coercion: No Right to Unilaterally Control Your Own Borders'. *Political Theory* 36 (1): 37–65.

Abrahamian, A. A. 2015. *The Cosmopolites: The Coming of the Global Citizen*. New York: Columbia Global Reports.

Anderson, B. 2013. *Us and Them?: The Dangerous Politics of Immigration Control*. Oxford: Oxford University Press.

Andersson, R. 2014. *Illegality, Inc.: Clandestine Migration and the Business of Bordering Europe*. Oakland, CA: University of California Press.

Arendt, H. 1958. *The Origins of Totalitarianism*, 2nd edn. London: George Allen & Unwin.

Bradley, B. 2012. 'Doing Away with Harm'. *Philosophy and Phenomenological Research* 85 (2): 390–412.

Carens, J. H. 1987. 'Aliens and Citizens: The Case for Open Borders'. *The Review of Politics* 49 (2): 251–73.

References

Carens, J. H. 2013. *The Ethics of Immigration*. Oxford: Oxford University Press.

Cole, P. 2000. *Philosophies of Exclusion: Liberal Political Theory and Immigration*. Edinburgh: Edinburgh University Press.

Dumitru, S. 2014. 'Qu'est-Ce Que Le Nationalisme Methodologique? Essai de Typologie'. *Raisons Politiques* 54 (2): 9–22.

Easterly, W. 2001. *The Elusive Quest for Growth*. Cambridge, MA: MIT Press.

Gibney, M. J. 2015. 'Refugees and Justice between States'. *European Journal of Political Theory* 14 (4): 448–63.

Griffiths, M. 2017. 'Foreign, Criminal: A Doubly Damned Modern British Folk-Devil'. *Citizenship Studies* 21 (5): 527–46.

Hathaway, J. C. and M. Foster. 2014. *The Law of Refugee Status*. Cambridge: Cambridge University Press.

Heath, J. 1997. 'Immigration, Multiculturalism, and the Social Contract'. *Canadian Journal of Law and Jurisprudence* 10 (2): 343–61.

Hidalgo, J. 2015. 'Resistance to Unjust Immigration Restrictions'. *Journal of Political Philosophy* 23 (4): 450–70.

Holtug, N. 2002. 'The Harm Principle'. *Ethical Theory and Moral Practice* 5 (4): 357–89.

Huemer, M. 2010. 'Is There a Right to Immigrate?' *Social Theory and Practice* 36 (3): 429–61.

Huemer, M. 2013. *The Problem of Political Authority*. Basingstoke: Palgrave Macmillan.

International Organization for Migration. 2015. *2015 Global Migration Trends Factsheet*. Berlin: International Organization for Migration Global Data Analysis Centre.

Jones, R. 2016. *Violent Borders: Refugees and the Right to Move*. London: Verso.

Joppke, C. 1999. *Immigration and the Nation-State: The United States, Germany, and Great Britain*. Oxford: Oxford University Press.

Judt, T. 2011. *Postwar: A History of Europe Since 1945*. New York: Random House.

Kant, I. 1996a. 'The Metaphysic of Morals'. In *Practical Philosophy*, edited by Mary J. Gregor. The Cambridge Edition of the Works of Immanuel Kant. Cambridge: Cambridge University Press.

Kant, I. 1996b. 'Toward Perpetual Peace'. In *Practical Philosophy*, edited by Mary J. Gregor. The Cambridge Edition of the Works of Immanuel Kant. Cambridge: Cambridge University Press.

Kleingeld, P. 2012. *Kant and Cosmopolitanism: The Philosophical Ideal of World Citizenship*. Cambridge: Cambridge University Press.

Lenard, P. T. 2010. 'Culture, Free Movement, and Open Borders'. *The Review of Politics* 72 (4): 627–52.

Mann, C. C. 2011. *1493: Uncovering the New World Columbus Created*. New York: Knopf.

Mendoza, J. J. 2015. 'Enforcement Matters: Reframing the Philosophical Debate over Immigration'. *Journal of Speculative Philosophy* 29 (1): 73–90.

Milanovic, B. 2016. *Global Inequality*. Cambridge, MA: Harvard University Press.

Miller, D. M. 2016. *Strangers in Our Midst*. Cambridge, MA: Harvard University Press.

Morris, C. W. 1998. *An Essay on the Modern State*. Cambridge: Cambridge University Press.

Murphy, L. 2000. *Moral Demands in Non-Ideal Theory*. Oxford: Oxford University Press.

Nussbaum, M. 2000. *Women and Human Development*. Cambridge: Cambridge University Press.

Ottonelli, V. and T. Torresi. 2010. 'Inclusivist Egalitarian Liberalism and Temporary Migration: A Dilemma'. *Journal of Political Philosophy* 20 (2): 202–24.

Owen, D. 2013. 'Citizenship and the Marginalities of Migrants'. *Critical Review of International Social and Political Philosophy* 16 (3): 326–43.

Prabhat, D. 2017. 'Political Context and Meaning of British Citizenship: Cancellation as a National Security Measure'. *Law, Culture and the Humanities*, https://doi.org/10.1177/1743872116655305.

Rawls, J. 1971. *A Theory of Justice*. Cambridge, MA: Harvard University Press.

Rawls, J. 1993. *The Law of Peoples*. Cambridge, MA: Harvard University Press.

Ripstein, A. 2009. *Force and Freedom: Kant's Legal*

and Political Philosophy. Cambridge, MA: Harvard University Press.

Roff, H. M. 2013. *Global Justice, Kant and the Responsibility to Protect: A Provisional Duty*. London: Taylor & Francis.

Sager, A. 2016a. 'Methodological Nationalism and the "Brain Drain"'. In A. Sager (ed.) *The Ethics and Politics of Immigration*. London: Rowman & Littlefield.

Sager, A. 2016b. 'Methodological Nationalism, Migration and Political Theory'. *Political Studies* 64 (1): 42–59.

Sager, A. 2017. 'Immigration Enforcement and Domination'. *Political Research Quarterly* 70 (1): 42–54.

Scott, J. C. 2009. *The Art of Not Being Governed: An Anarchist History of Upland Southeast Asia*. New Haven, CT: Yale University Press.

Shachar, A. 2009. *The Birthright Lottery: Citizenship and Global Inequality*. Cambridge, MA: Harvard University Press.

Stemplowska, Z. 2016. 'Doing More Than One's Fair Share'. *Critical Review of International Social and Political Philosophy* 19 (5): 591–608.

Walzer, M. 1983. *Spheres of Justice: A Defence of Pluralism and Equality*. New York: Basil Blackwell.

Wellman, C. H. 2008. 'Immigration and Freedom of Association'. *Ethics* 119 (1): 109–41.

Wellman, C. H. and P. Cole. 2011. *Debating the Ethics*

of Immigration: Is There a Right to Exclude? New York: Oxford University Press.

Wray, H. 2011. *Regulating Marriage Migration into the UK: A Stranger in the Home.* Farnham: Ashgate.

Ypi, L. 2012. 'A Permissive Theory of Territorial Rights'. *European Journal of Philosophy* 22 (2): 288–312.